Lacrosse Fundamentals

Second Edition

Lacrosse Fundamentals

Second Edition

Jim Hinkson

Warwick Publishing
Toronto Chicago

This book is dedicated to my wife Cynndy
for her great support

and to my children, of whom I am so proud,
Maggie, Katie, and James

— • —

The publisher wishes to thank LACROSSE INTERNATIONAL, the Canadian distributor of BRINE LACROSSE and the manufacturer of REBEL sporting equipment, for their generous sponsorship of this book.

Lacrosse Fundamentals
©1993, 2000 Jim Hinkson
Second Edition, April 2000

We acknowledge the financial support of the Government of Canada through the Book Publishing Industry Development Program for our publishing activities.

ISBN: 1-895629-11-X

Published by
Warwick Publishing
162 John Street, Toronto, Ontario M5V 2E5
Canada
www.warwickgp.com

Distributed in the United States by:
LPC Group
1436 West Randolph Street
Chicago, Illinois 60607

Distributed in Canada by:
General Distribution Services Ltd.
325 Humber College Blvd.
Toronto, ON M9W 7C3

Interior Photographs: Dieter Hessel
Cover Photographs: Dan Hamilton
Editor: Melinda Tate

Printed and bound in Canada

Table of Contents

Chapter 11 — Goaltending. . . . 165

Key to Diagrams

◯ = player

⬤ = ballcarrier

Ⓡ = right-shot player

Ⓛ = left-shot player

G = Goalie

C = Coach

Ⓧ = Pylon

△ = Net

⟶ = path of player

- - - -▸ = path of ball

〰〰▸ = path of ballcarrier

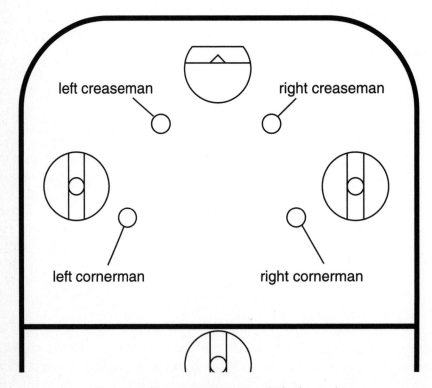

left creaseman

right creaseman

left cornerman

right cornerman

Note: Right creaseman is a left-shot player.

Foreword

LACROSSE is more than a game among members of my family and among the families of the Longhouse on the Territory of the Onondaga Nation.

I remember the first time that my father and I played catch. I was about five years old when he asked me to come out with him. He handed me a lacrosse stick and a ball. He showed me how to throw the ball. We played catch. That day, although it was over 55 years ago, is still in my mind as if it were yesterday.

I received my first stick when I was about 10 years old. It was made of white ash and was the stick that I used until it broke during a game when I was 17 years old. I played league lacrosse until I was 41.

During those years, I learned what the game really meant. I watched my father as he prepared to leave for his games in arenas in Syracuse, Geneva, and Rochester, New York. He played professional box lacrosse during the thirties. He also played field lacrosse against the colleges in our area. His team was good enough to try out for the 1932 Olympics in California. My grandfather played field lacrosse until he was 60 years old. My three sons have also played box and field lacrosse. Each has had a stick in his hands since he was two years old. One is presently playing for a college and one played pro box with the Buffalo Bandits. All three have played high school lacrosse and all three play for the Iroquois Nationals, a team composed of members of the Haudenosaunee (Iroquois Confederacy). Someone from my family has been on the lacrosse field for the past 100 years.

As my boys grew up I taught them the same respect for the game that my father had taught me. The game was given to us by the Creator for his enjoyment. We believe that when there is a game being played here on Earth there is a game being played in the land of the Creator at the same time. The game is for the spiritual and physical peace of mind of our people and gives us the chance to display our gifts for the Creator: the gifts of being able to run, catch, and throw; of being able to think and make split-second decisions; and most importantly, it gives us the opportunity to work together as a unit.

Lacrosse is a very intrinsic component of our heritage and spiritual culture. When I play lacrosse it makes me feel like I am playing the game with all of my ancestors. It also makes me proud that it was our people who gave lacrosse to the world. For these reasons, lacrosse is more than just a game.

Dawnaytoh

Chief Irving Powless, Jr.

Onondaga Nation

Preface

THIS book is an accumulation of my ideas from 30 years of experience playing, coaching, and instructing for the Ontario Lacrosse Association.

I was introduced to lacrosse in 1962 by Hall of Famer Jim Bishop, who knew only one way to play the game: to Fast-Break. From these special roots, I've grown and added my own ideas about how to play.

Lacrosse may be known by different names — Box Lacrosse, Indoor Lacrosse, Inter-Lacrosse, and Field Lacrosse — and may be played in different environments with different rules. But the bottom line is that in all these different forms, a player still has to pass and catch, beat a defender, and shoot at a net, with only a lacrosse stick and a ball.

Lacrosse is a very simple game; its object—to put the ball in the net. It is a game of tempo and rhythm with two teams running the floor, yet like all sports, it is a game made up of fundamentals. It's through repetitive practice of these fundamental skills that teams become successful. There is an old saying: "It's not what you do, but how you do it." In lacrosse, this translates to, "The type of system a team plays is not as important as how well a team executes the fundamental skills within that system."

The execution of these fundamentals is presented in this book: how to beat a defender one-on-one; how to throw the perfect pass to a teammate; how to catch a ball in traffic; how to score on a goalie; and many others.

I've tried to describe the fundamentals as clearly and simply as possible. I've tried to break the skills down into a checklist of key points. Rmemeber: these fundamentals are not just any fundamentals thrown together, but ones that complement the Fast-Break system. So, as you read, keep in mind that I'm giving you one proven method. Take from the book ideas that you can use, and feel good about the ideas that reinforce what you are doing already.

I've also presented some basic strategies and tips on how players should think and act in certain situations. Most of the chapters provide drills, which are presented in simple step-by-step progressions from the easiest to the most difficult. Practicing these drills will refine a player's skills. By breaking the game down into basic skills, the player, coach, and fan can analyze and thereby better understand and appreciate theis great sport.

Finally, a special note to parents: This book is written not only for the player, coach and educator, but also for you. It's a tool for parents who want to work with their sons and daughters on their own time. Even if you can't handle a lacrosse stick, take this book and the ideas presented in it, grab a baseball glove and practice passing and catching with your child. Having a stick yourself isn't essential; understanding skills and techniques of the game is.

Preface to the Second Edition

Having been involved with the St. Catharines Majors during the summer of 1999, and then with the National Lacrosse League (N.L.L.) as a coach with the New York Saints, the one thing that stands out for me is that it doesn't matter what system a player plays. The outstanding players are good because they are strong in the basic skills of lacrosse, which they have developed through years of practicing the little things.

As in any sport, there are many changes going on in lacrosse, and I have tried to accommodate many of them here. The wooden stick has pretty well become a thing of the past, except for the wooden goalie stick. And many elements of the field game have entered into our box game, such as the offense-defense system, beating a man with one hand on the stick, and the wrap-around check. The size of the net has also been increased to $4^1/2$ feet by 4 feet (1.37 m x 1.22 m). In fact, there is talk of the nets going to 4 by 5 ft. (1.22 x 1.52 m) in the N.L.L. next year. Due to this changeability and the fact that different leagues have different rules, it is important to consult a current rule book for your league to confirm that the moves I describe are permissible in your situation.

Lastly, I don't want to be seen as politically incorrect by talking about just the male person all the time in this book, but the reality is, box lacrosse is still played mostly by males. Some females may play minor box lacrosse, but usually only as an entrance into girls' field lacrosse. Most girls play field lacrosse — I have two daughters who played it — and the fundamentals of that game are totally different from those of the male-dominated box lacrosse I deal with here. I don't know too much about that other game, so I will leave girls' field lacrosse to the women who know more about it than I do.

I'm really happy we did this second edition of *Lacrosse Fundamentals*, as it gives me a chance to improve on the first version and add some new ideas I've picked up over the past few years dealing with some of the greatest players in the field and box games. It is certainly a privilege to be involved in lacrosse, and especially in the N.L.L.

Introduction

Like most Canadian youngsters, I played lacrosse and hockey. The speed, the keen competition, the sheer exuberance of these sports allowed for the development of athleticism in a young boy. As I grew older, I began to recognize the tactics and strategies of these games; I became a student of sports.

Later, as a teacher and a coach, I tried to channel those spirits in my students, to impart to them the elementary rules, to instill in them a love of the game and respect for the opponent. Teaching fundamentals, increasing knowledge without destroying or limiting one's enthusiasm for a subject, is sometimes difficult for a teacher and a coach to accomplish.

In a sport like lacrosse there is a continuous movement, a flow that exhilarates the player and arouses the spectator. It is difficult to take that energy and slow it down to examine its creation. A step-by-step re-creation of the fundamentals is needed — like watching a film in slow motion to capture the subtleties of each player's abilities. We watch every move; we observe the hand-to-eyes coordination needed to succeed in this sport. Jim Hinkson has known the ebb and flow of such play and has put it into words, using instructional photographs and diagrams to complement them.

This book is designed to benefit everyone: the coach, the player, and the spectator. It puts in concrete terms the manner in which the sport works, purely and simply. It will make a player more aware, a coach more expert, a spectator more informed. Lacrosse Fundamentals will inform everyone who reads it — each individual can take it from there.

Knowing Jim Hinkson as a player, teacher, and coach, and knowing his dedication to the sport of lacrosse, I wholeheartedly recommend this book to you.

Mike Keenan
Former Coach of the New York Rangers, Philadelphia Flyers, Chicago Black Hawks, Vancouver Canucks, and St. Louis Blues

Parts of the Stick

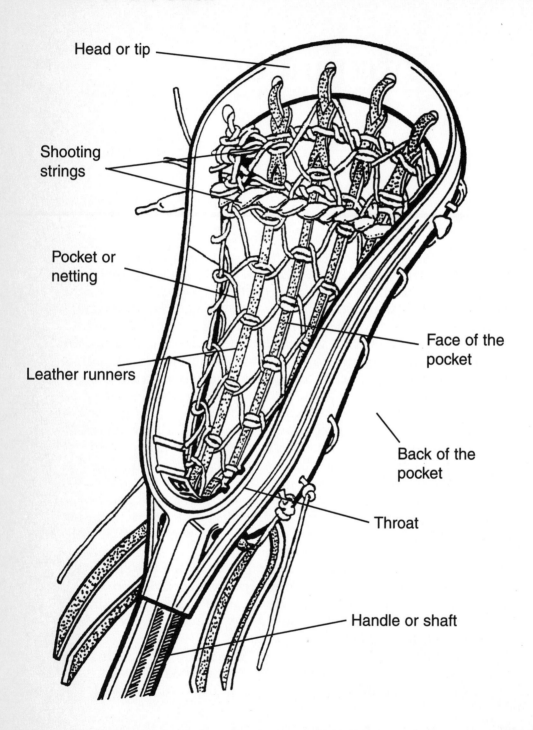

Head or tip

Shooting strings

Pocket or netting

Leather runners

Face of the pocket

Back of the pocket

Throat

Handle or shaft

— 1 —
The Stick

MANY coaches do not take the time to talk about the stick, yet it is like a carpenter's tool: the better the tool, the easier it is to work with. So coaches should spend some time going over the finer points of the stick with players.

In the first edition of this book I discussed both the plastic stick and the traditional wooden stick. The plastic stick is lighter and therefore easier to handle, especially for younger players. It is also easier to scoop up loose balls with the plastic stick because of its sharp, pointed mouth. For these and other reasons, the traditional wooden stick has became virtually extinct in the last few years, so I will now limit my discussion here to the plastic version.

I. Parts of the Stick

- Butt or end
- Handle or shaft
- Throat
- Head or tip
- Face of the pocket
- Back of the pocket
- Pocket or netting
- Leather runners
- Shooting strings

II. Customizing the Stick

Netting

There are two types of netting. Most players prefer the all-mesh netting, since it doesn't need breaking in. Also, the mesh has no up-keep. However, although the mesh netting is the most commonly used netting, it does not control and absorb the ball as well as leather-runner netting. With mesh it is easier to knock the ball out of the stick and harder to catch with it because the ball tends to bounce out more often.

Therefore, some players prefer the combination of cord netting with leather runners. This combination is very easy to break in, and the ball releases quickly from the pocket, thus complementing the Fast-Break System of play.

Players who use the cord netting with leather runners feel it produces a more accurate pass and shot, and makes it easier to control and absorb the ball in the stick, especially when catching. It also gives the player a better "feel" for the ball. The only drawbacks of the cord netting–leather runner combination are that it takes time to soften up to form a pocket, it can break after repeated use, and a player has to constantly play with the leather runners by pulling them in or letting them out to get a smooth pocket.

Length of the Stick

The official rule is that a stick should be between 42 and 46 inches (107–117 cm) in length for players over 12 years of age. Most players feel that the shorter the stick, the better they can control it, so they like to cut the stick near the 43-inch (109-cm) mark.

Depth of the Pocket

The depth of the pocket depends on the type of system a player plays in and the type of shooter he is.

Usually, in a Ball-Control System the pockets are fairly deep because of the higher frequency of one-on-one situations where you don't want to cough up the ball easily. In the Fast-Break System, the pockets are not as deep; the criterion is usually that one should just see the top of the ball under the bottom of the frame. This type of pocket gives a player the ability to pass the ball much more quickly, as the Fast-Break System requires.

A few players like to have very shallow pockets, almost as flat as a tennis racquet. Most overhand shooters have average-depth pockets (i.e., a ball-width deep or less), while sidearm and underhand shooters like depths of a ball or more.

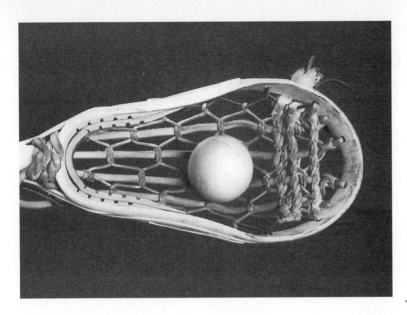

Photo 1:
The pocket of
a lacrosse
stick seen
from above

Forming the Shooting Pocket

Players should catch and throw from the same spot in the netting all the time. Usually this spot, called the "Shooting Pocket," is found at the edge of the last shooting string near the tip of the stick. It is best to form the shooting pocket just below the last shooting string so there is a nice, short, smooth path for the ball to run out of.

With the ball resting against the last shooting string, a player has a quicker release and more momentum in his shot. It also gives the ball a higher trajectory and thereby less chance of "hooking" — hitting the original shooting string and consequently going low.

If the shooting pocket is at the back of the netting, i.e. near the throat of the stick, the ball has too far to run and by the time it exits the pocket the head of the stick is in front of the player's body, resulting in a low pass.

The plastic stick is made for the field game, with the pocket automatically formed at the throat of the stick. The shape and structure of the plastic stick makes it very easy and natural to form the pocket at the throat of the stick, with the result that the ball is released low and slow. This is completely opposite to what is needed for the box lacrosse game, which requires forming the pocket at the tip of the stick.

Box lacrosse players must work at forming their pocket at the tip of the plastic stick even before they use it. This is accomplished by pulling the mesh tight at the throat of the stick and letting out the cord holding the mesh along the side of the frame to form the pocket at the tip.

Often in a game, overhand players catch the ball by accident in the middle of the pocket rather than in the tip. Two ways to get the ball to the tip of the stick are to cradle the ball to the tip (see chapter 2), and/or to drop the head of the stick so the ball will roll down to the tip.

Overhand passers can pass and shoot the ball from close to the tip of the stick because of its shallow pocket, while sidearm and underhand shooters need deep pockets to keep the ball in the stick. They use four to five shooting strings to give a smooth path for the ball to come out of the pocket. Because of this, the shooting pocket ends up in the middle of the stick.

For the overhand passer the ball should sit in the dead center of the two bottom runners to create a path for the ball to come straight out of the pocket. This again complements the "straight-line" theory in teaching overhand passing (see chapter 4). Sidearm and underhand shooters, especially left-handers, like the ball to rest against the side frame. They feel this is a better position for shooting and faking.

Shooting Strings

Shooting strings help to raise the mesh so that the ball does not hit or get caught in the plastic tip. It is important when intertwining the shooting strings to secure them to both sides of the plastic frame to give stability.

When passing the ball, it's important to avoid "hooking." A stick hooks when the exiting ball hits the permanent shooting string that comes with the stick, or hits extra shooting strings added by the player that are too tight or too loose, thus changing the direction of the ball as it leaves the pocket and forcing it down.

Players put in extra shooting strings to make a smooth path for the ball to run out of the pocket. Heavy skate laces are intertwined and attached to the frame to raise the netting slightly. Only one to two laces are normally used, but sidehand and underhand shooters could use up to five.

> **Note** *Make sure shooting strings are tied to both sides of the frame to keep the strings secure and stable.*

The important thing to remember is that shooting strings should be put in a stick for a reason — which is, to create a smooth path for the ball to run out of, or to get rid of a hook. Once the shooting strings are in place, the player should always be checking the roll of the ball over them to make sure the ball's path is smooth. If there is a ridge or gully created by the shooting strings, they should be tightened or loosened as needed.

The Handle

Besides cutting the handle to make it a comfortable length, its shape can also be altered to suit the player's style, or to retain some of the attributes of the old wooden sticks.

The metal handle of the plastic stick can be adjusted to make it feel like a traditional wooden handle by bending it where the top-hand grabs the stick or about a third of the distance of the shaft from the end of the handle. Putting a curve on the handle places the head of the stick farther behind one's back to make the shot more deceptive for a goalie and makes the handle feel like a traditional wooden stick.

- Tape the entire aluminum handle to give it the feel of a traditional wooden stick.
- Stuff the aluminum handle with a long, round, small piece of wood to give it weight and more support.
- Cut down a defensive field stick, use a goalie's aluminum handle, or use a graphite handle, which all are a heavier grade of aluminum.

An overhand passer likes the handle to line up in the middle of the tip so that the stick is balanced, again in accord with the straight-line theory of passing.

The Head of the Stick

The mouth of the stick can be widened or narrowed according to the player's preference. The trade-off for a narrow-mouth stick is that the ball comes out more accurately, but the narrow shape makes catching slightly more difficult.

Make the plastic head narrower for better control by unstringing the head and heating it in the oven:

1. Before heating the head, wrap wire or string through the middle holes in the head to make it easier to handle the head when it is cooling.

2. Place the head in the oven for 10 minutes at around 350°F (175°C). Or put the head in the microwave for 30 seconds with the power on a high setting. (If using microwave do not use metal wire to wrap the head!) Heat the head until it becomes soft.

3. When it is soft, squeeze the head, making it narrower, and wrap wire around it until it cools off. It is important to string the wire over both the top and bottom of the head to ensure that the walls remain straight. It is also a good idea to stuff the throat of the heated head with the heel of an old shoe to make sure the throat remains a consistent width (3-4"/7.5-10 cm) and does not become too thin.

4. Let the heated stick cool for about 30 minutes before attempting to string it. Some players drill the plastic holes along the side of the frame and near the tip to make them big enough to allow both the shooting string and the cord that holds the netting to the frame to go through.

Gripping the Stick

The beginning lacrosse player will probably need to practice a bit with a stick before he starts making adaptations to it; he has to find out what is comfortable and suitable for him by cradling, catching and passing the ball, skills which will be covered in the next few chapters.

Before moving on to learning these skills, however, the player should know the proper way to grip the lacrosse stick. A player shouldn't grab the lacrosse stick like he would a hockey stick or an axe. The stick should be held loosely with the fingers to get fingertip control. A player wants this loose grip to get a good feel of the stick. Also, holding the stick with the fingers helps to keep the wrists flexible to rotate the stick when cradling and faking. Some players like to place their thumbs up along the shaft to get a better feel of the stick and to give the wrists more flexibility.

The bottom hand is placed at the butt of the stick, holding the stick lightly so it can rotate in the hand. The top hand is placed slightly below the midpoint of the shaft, about eight inches (20 cm) from the bottom hand. This is usually the balance point of a stick.

Another way to determine the placement of the top hand is to grab the stick roughly in the middle of the shaft with the top hand only, making sure the butt of the stick is touching the elbow. Wherever the top hand ends up with the elbow touching the butt is a good placement for the top hand.

The closeness of the hands makes it easier to control the stick for faking, passing, and shooting. If a player grabs his stick too high on the shaft, the passing becomes jerky and he cannot complete his follow-through. If a player's top hand is too close to his bottom hand, he will not have good control of the head of his stick.

— 2 —
Cradling

CRADLING should be the first skill to teach and master in lacrosse.

I. What Is Cradling?

Cradling is a side-to-side, back-and-forth, or up-and-down rocking motion of the stick which

- keeps the ball in a player's stick and gives him the ability to run and get checked with the ball and still hang on to it;
- tells a player by "feel" or by weight if the ball is in his stick; and
- tells a player where the ball is in his pocket without having to look at it.

II. When to Cradle

Basically, a player cradles whenever he has the ball; the stick should never be stationary when the ball is in the stick, particularly

- when taking a check;
- when running down the floor with the ball;
- when protecting the stick after obtaining a loose ball;
- when getting the ball to the tip of the stick for a shot or a pass;
- when checking by feel to see if the ball is still in the stick; and
- when unsure where the ball is in the pocket.

III. Position of the Stick When Cradling

The four positions of holding the stick for cradling are:

1. High at a 45-degree angle to the floor just before passing or shooting (see chapters 4 and 9 for more on passing and shooting).

2. High and horizontally in a cocked position just before passing or shooting.

3. At waist level and horizontally while running up the floor. Most players have a natural tendency to run with the ball carrying it at waist level, but it is more practical to run with the ball while holding the stick up in a passing position.

4. Vertically or at a slight 45-degree angle beside the body while taking a check (see chapter 8 for more about individual defense).

IV. Three Types of Cradles

Different types of cradles are used in different situations. The main thing differentiating each type is the size of the arc in the cradle's swinging motion.

A. The Small Cradle

The small cradle is used when passing, stationary or when shooting. The stick is in a "cocked" position — horizontal to the floor. This small, side-to-side or

Photo 2:
The small
cradle

up-and-down shaking motion of the stick is used when a player wants to know where the ball is in the stick or when moving the ball to the tip of the stick for a shot or a pass.

This continuous swinging or shaking action is mainly accomplished by the top-hand wrist, usually when the stick is held in the "cocked" position, i.e., horizontal to the floor. The top-hand wrist rotates either side to side, causing the stick to rock side to side, or up and down, causing the stick to swing up and down.

This swinging or shaking motion helps a player "feel" the weight of the ball in the pocket and move it to the tip of the pocket.

> **Note**   *The hand placements are as described in "Gripping the Stick" in chapter 1. The butt of the stick turns in the bottom-hand grip.*

B. The Medium Cradle

The medium cradle consists more of an up-and-down motion of the stick than the small cradle. It is used when running down the floor with the ball in "heavy traffic" to let the player know by "feel" that he has the ball. Its swinging motion also creates a centrifugal force to help keep the ball in the stick. The stick is held horizontally in front of the body with two hands.

The top-hand wrist does most of the work in the medium cradle: while

*Photo 3:
The medium
cradle*

holding the shaft mainly with the fingers, straighten the fingers and let the stick roll downwards to the fingertips, then curl the fingers and the wrist upwards, bringing the stick up also.

The medium cradle is created by the top-hand wrist motion and the forearm moving simultaneously upwards and downwards. The hand placements are wider than those of the standard grip — the top-hand holds the shaft near the throat of the stick and the bottom-hand grips the butt. The stick turns in the bottom-hand grip.

C. The Large Cradle

This back-and-forth rocking action of the stick is mainly used when taking a cross-check while carrying the ball. If a player merely holds the ball in the pocket when taking a check, the ball will simply be jarred out by the sudden impact of the cross-check. The large cradle can prevent this from happening.

The stick is held vertically to the floor. The continuous back-and-forth swinging motion of the stick is created by the wrist, the forearm, and the upper arm of the top-hand moving forward and backward. It is important that the top-hand grips the stick at the throat. This motion of the wrist and forearm, as noted below, creates a force keeping the ball in the stick. The bottom-hand grip at the butt is loose, allowing the stick to rotate within it. On contact from the cross-check, make sure the top-hand wrist is rotating forward. This will put the face of the pocket in the direction of the impact, so that the pocket netting will block the ball from falling out *(see photo 4 below)*.

Photo 4:
The large
cradle

Note   *With all three cradles, the bottom hand grips the stick at the butt. The only hand that moves is the top hand, according to the type of cradle.*

Points to Stress about Taking a Check:

- Just before going one-on-one, hold the stick in front of your stomach horizontally

- Turn your body sideways as a shield to protect the stick, and take the impact on the upper arm padding rather than on the back. Swing your stick up vertically.

- Keep your head up; look at the net or the checker over your shoulder rather than the ball in the stick.

- Choke up on the stick (hold it at the throat) to cradle better.

- Hold the stick vertically while executing the large cradle. Never keep the stick stationary when in possession of the ball.

- Lean into the check but keep your body relaxed. By relaxing, you create dead-weight which makes it easier to cradle the ball. Resisting a cross-check is counterproductive; if you tense up there's a better chance of the ball being jarred loose.

- Take a wide stance to keep good balance and stability on the hit.

See chapter 8 for more tips on taking a check.

Box Dimensions

12-15'

30'

16'

6'

9'

180-200'

11'

10'

change area

4'

2'

8'

— 3 —
Catching

STICKHANDLING or ballhandling is the ability to catch and throw the ball accurately without a conscious effort and without looking at the ball when it is in the stick.

Catching is part of ballhandling, which is based on the "feel" or weight of the ball in the stick. For beginners, catching (the "give") is a much harder skill to master than passing, so more attention should be paid to this skill for those new to lacrosse.

There are five main components of catching the ball cleanly:

   I. Grip

  II. Receiving Position of Stick

 III. Contact of the Ball with the Netting

 IV. Eye on the Ball

  V. The Catch

I. Grip

Hand Position

The bottom hand, which gives the stick stability and holds it vertically, is placed at the butt of the stick, holding the stick lightly so it can rotate in the hand.

Hold the stick with the fingers — don't grab the stick — placing the thumbs along the shaft.

Photo 5:
The catching
grip

The top hand is for power and for guiding the stick when passing. It is placed slightly below the mid-point of the shaft, about eight inches (20 cm) from the bottom hand (see Photo 6 on p. 30).

Loosen Grip

Players should be loose with the grip when catching; the wrist and fingers of both hands need to be relaxed. If a player tightens up with his hands and arms, he will be stiff and rigid in his passing and catching. He will be "fighting" the ball when trying to move his stick quickly to get it in front of the ball.

Using Thumbs

Some players like to place both their thumbs along the shaft to have more control and flexibility with the stick.

From Catching to Passing

Experienced players should not have to move their top hand up the shaft to catch and then move it down to pass; their hands should remain stationary. But beginning players who are having problems catching can slide the top hand up the shaft to the throat to catch, then slide it back down to pass.

II. Receiving Position of Stick

Provide a Good Target

The "face" of the pocket should be lined up to the passer so that he has a good target to aim at.

Stance

The receiver faces the passer and hold his stick out in front, about one foot (30 cm) from his body, and above his shoulder. By holding the stick in front of him, rather than at the side of his body, the receiver can catch the ball and see the play in front of him developing. In addition, the stick is in a good position to "give" with the contact of the ball, and it is easier to line up the face of the stick with the oncoming ball.

Ideally, a pass should be received high over the receiver's stick shoulder so that he will be ready to shoot or pass immediately upon receiving the ball.

Receiving

Line up the face of the pocket in front of the ball and let the ball come to the pocket.

From Catching to Throwing

It is important that the receiver catch the ball with the stick in the same position as he would throw from. It is also important to catch the ball in the same spot (the tip) in the pocket that he throws from. Both these techniques allow a quick release and do not waste time in cocking or cradling the stick before passing or shooting.

Be Prepared

It is very important to be physically and mentally prepared to pass the ball even before catching it. The receiver should be holding his stick in a passing position so that as soon as he catches the ball he is in a position to pass it. Have the stick up and ready!

*Photos 6, 7
& 8:
The receiving
position of
the stick —
receiving;
contact;
caught.*

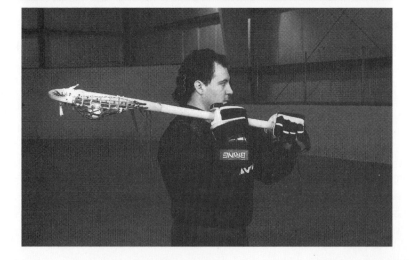

III. Contact of Ball with Netting — The "Clean" Catch

Before Contact

Before contact with the ball, the receiver keeps the stick out in front of his body and waits for the ball to come to the stick. As the ball approaches the pocket, he drops the stick gradually back.

Players should avoid "reaching" when receiving the ball. Reaching for the ball with his stick forces the player to cradle the stick by automatically bringing the stick around in front of his body so the ball will not fall out of the pocket. This movement wastes time, especially when executing a quick give-and-go play, because once he catches the ball, the player has to take his stick back to get it in a cocked position to pass.

On Contact

Upon the actual contact of the ball with the netting, the stick should be beside the receiver's head.

Impact

Similar to catching a baseball in a glove, the receiver must "give" with his stick upon the impact of the ball — he should slow the ball down gradually. He "gives" by relaxing his top-hand arm and wrist. This motion lets his stick head drop backwards as it makes contact with the ball and helps to cushion the impact of the ball in the pocket so that it will not bounce out. Players should think of catching the ball the same way they would catch an egg.

Errors to Watch For When Learning How to Catch

Beginning players have a tendency to make certain common errors:

- they tighten up or "fight the ball" when catching;
- they try to catch the ball in front of their body by trying to stop the ball immediately, with the result that the ball bounces out of their stick (this is the most common error when learning to catch); and
- they twirl their stick inwards to help keep the ball in the pocket

IV. Eye on the Ball

When catching, players should concentrate on keeping an eye on the ball as it approaches them. Players often drop passes because of a lack of concentration.

A beginner may have to watch the ball until it's in the pocket, but once it's in his stick, he can watch the play.

V. The Catch

Once the ball is caught, the pocket of the stick should be in a horizontal position or slightly higher so the ball does not roll out.

Now the player is prepared to pass or shoot the ball.

Photo 9:
After Catching — *the cradling position prior to passing or shooting*

— 4 —

Passing

CATCHING and passing are the most important fundamentals in lacrosse! If teams can't pass and catch accurately and quickly they then must rely strictly on one-on-one ballhandling, in which case the defensive team would have an easy time stopping the ballcarrier knowing the team can't pass and catch. Be sure to spend adequate time mastering passing and catching skills.

There are six components of the perfect overhand pass:

   I. Stance or Ready Position
  II. Grip of Stick
 III. Cradling Position of Stick Prior to Pass
 IV. Cocked Position of Stick
  V. Throwing Motion
 VI. Follow-through of Stick

I. Stance or Ready Position

Upon catching the ball, the receiver turns his body from facing the passer to a sideways stance, like a baseball batter's stance, with his front shoulder facing his target and his front foot forward. This is usually the stance taken in a game as the ballcarrier is likely being checked and must protect his stick with his body by turning it sideways.

II. Grip of Stick

Again, the stick is held loosely with the fingers to get fingertip control. A player wants this loose grip to get a good feel of the stick. Also, holding the stick with the fingers helps to keep the wrists flexible to rotate the stick when cradling and faking. Some players like to place their thumbs up along the shaft to get a better feel of the stick and to give the wrists more flexibility.

REMEMBER: The bottom hand is placed at the butt of the stick, holding the stick lightly so it can rotate in the hand.

The top hand is placed slightly below the mid-point of the shaft, about eight inches (20 cm) from the bottom hand. This is usually the balance point of a stick.

Another way to determine the placement of the top hand is to grab the stick roughly in the middle of the shaft, with the top hand only, making sure the butt of the stick is touching the elbow. Wherever the top hand ends up with the elbow touching the butt is a good placement for the top hand.

The closeness of the hands makes it easier to control the stick for faking, passing, and shooting. If a player grabs his stick too high on the shaft, the passing becomes jerky and he cannot complete his follow-through. If a player's top hand is too close to his bottom hand, he will not have good control of the head of his stick.

III. Cradling Position of Stick Prior to Pass

The player holds his stick straight up and down at a slight 45-degree angle over his stick shoulder while doing a small cradle with the ball (see chapter 2 on cradling).

The top hand holds the shaft beside the player's head while the bottom hand holds the butt of the stick below the top hand, putting the stick in a vertical position.

A player keeps the stick close to, but not touching his body, with the arms slightly flexed to protect it and to help move it more quickly from this position.

IV. Cocked Position of Stick

A player cocks his stick when he is getting ready to pass or throw the ball. As a player cocks his wrists backwards, his top-hand arm moves his stick straight back, with the butt of his stick pointing at his target. This horizontal position of the stick, plus the body weight on the back foot, puts the player in a good passing position. Some players like to hold their stick at a 45-degree angle to

The Throwing Motion

Photos 10, 11: cocked position and follow-through

the floor rather than horizontally, but this depends on what is comfortable for each individual player.

V. Throwing Motion

The player should always start the throw off his back foot, then take a short, six-inch (12-cm) step with his front foot to help transfer his weight from the back foot to the front foot. "Stepping into the pass" in this way helps put more power into the pass. A player should be certain he steps with the foot opposite to his stick side. In some situations, for a quicker pass, players may have to stay stationary — take no step — and rely strictly on their arm action to make the pass.

At the same time as the player steps or shifts his weight forward, his stick is brought straight forward by his top-hand arm, and both cocked wrists are snapped forward.

When passing and catching, a good ballhandler will keep both hands stationary, about eight inches (20 cm) apart. Some players prefer to slide the top hand down the shaft during the actual passing motion.

It's important to find the point at which to release the ball from the pocket to get the perfect level on the pass. One of the main passing rules is to release the ball soon, not late from the stick. Releasing the ball from the stick while it is still behind the player's head makes the ball come out high rather than low. The ball leaving the stick from the tip of the pocket also helps to produce this high trajectory.

REMEMBER: The receiver is holding his stick high above his head in a position ready to pass or shoot the ball.

VI. Follow-through of Stick

- After the ball is released, the top-hand arm should end up fully extended, while the bottom-hand arm should remain flexed. Many beginners make the mistake of trying to push the ball out of the stick by extending both their arms fully, rather than using just the top arm.

- The butt end of the stick touches the elbow of the top hand to stress the ideal overhand pass.

- The tip of the stick points at the target, following the ball.

- The follow-through of the stick is straight ahead and down. The passer should not follow through across his body.

- The player's upper body is turned from a sideways position to end up facing his target (i.e., shoulders ending up square to the target).

- The body weight ends up on the front foot after the release.

In putting all the parts of the passing process together, stress throwing a natural, continuous, smooth, overhand throwing motion. The stick traces out the path of the top half of a Ferris wheel from the beginning of the pass to the end of the pass (i.e., the stick starts in a horizontal position to the floor and during the throwing phase flows a straight line forward ending up again horizontal to the floor). This "straight line" theory makes the overhand pass the simplest and most accurate pass there is.

Besides the motion of the top half of a Ferris wheel, other useful analogies for illustrating the correct overhead pass are the swinging action of an ax or the throwing motion in baseball.

Note *Although I've described the lacrosse player taking a baseball batter's stance to pass, he should not hold his stick the way a baseball player would hold a bat. A beginning player has a tendency to use the same motion as swinging a bat in baseball when throwing in lacrosse, thereby throwing the ball sidearm rather than overhand. Watch out for this and correct it when you see it.*

VII. Correcting the "Hook"

Every player, whether experienced or beginner, sometime in his lacrosse career "hooks" the ball in his stick, meaning the ball comes out of the stick at an unintended low trajectory, resulting in either the ball hitting the floor or heading towards the receiver's stomach area rather than his stick.

The hook may be caused by

- sloppy netting,
- the way the player throws the ball,
- the ball hitting the standard shooting string that comes with the stick,
- the location of the shooting pocket, or
- a pocket that is just too deep.

A player can correct the hooking problem by forcing the ball to be released higher. He does this by doing one or all of the following:

- smoothing out the pocket, especially making sure the runners are smooth and tight, not bulky;
- pulling in the runners to make the pocket shallower;
- putting in extra shooting strings to help the ball roll out of the netting smoothly while not hitting the permanent shooting string;
- making sure the shooting pocket is at the tip of the stick rather than in the middle or at the back of the pocket near the throat of the stick;
- releasing the ball from the stick when it is still behind the player's body rather than when the ball is beside or in front of his body.

Photo 12:
Passing to a
teammate on
the run

Tips for Passing

- Use the overhand pass only. It is the most accurate of all passes and it carries over into the overhand shot nicely.

- Before passing, make sure the receiver is looking and is ready for the pass. Eye contact is a good way to signal for a pass.

- Stress a "shooting" pass or a "passing" pass. This is a pass in which a player has only to catch and pass in one continuous motion. He does not have to move his stick from a catching position to another position for throwing or shooting.

- Pass with a snap of the wrist. Wrist passers have more accuracy and more power in their passes than "pushers" do.

- Throw hard, crisp passes, but not too hard. Passes are meant to be caught! Remember: it takes two to make a pass — a passer and a receiver. Most of the responsibility for a completed pass rests with the passer, however, and how accurate and hard he throws the ball. The hardness depends on whether his receiver is a good or poor receiver, and how far away his receiver is. It seems great passers have a certain softness to their pass that makes it catchable.

- Throw passes that are parallel to the floor. Avoid semi-lob or "rainbow" passes — also known as "suicide" passes — in a game. These passes move slowly, and when they finally reach the receiver his defender may have had time to set him up for an unsuspecting, hard cross-check! The only occasions for these last-resort passes are when throwing to a player who has a breakaway, or throwing to a player up the sideboards on his own side of the floor.

- Do not throw bounce passes, since they may take a bad bounce or come off the floor with back spin and sometimes spin out of the receiver's stick.

- Throw only short passes in the breakout and in the offense. The short pass is more accurate and therefore there are fewer chances for dropped balls and interceptions.

- Stress quick passes and quick releases, but not hurrying the pass. By hurrying, a player might pass too quickly, pass out of control, pass off balance, or make wrong decisions — any of which could cause bad passes.

- Emphasize accuracy over speed; pass quickly, but do not sacrifice accuracy. A great passer is accurate. He can pass right to the stick's head target. It doesn't matter how hard he can throw. What matters is how accurate he can throw. Power is nothing without control.

- Learn to use peripheral vision when passing. Avoid "telegraphing" passes — looking directly where you want to pass. Learn to be deceptive by faking a pass one way and passing the other way.

- Concentrate on the head of the stick as the target. Aim for a high outside pass on the receiver's stick side.

- Know what a perfect pass is: A pass into a receiver's stick without his having to move it.

- If a player makes a mistake on the height of a pass, the rule is, pass too high rather than too low. This rule is used because most players make the mistake of passing low too often. Therefore, this rule forces players to concentrate on throwing a high pass.

- The timing on throwing to a teammate on the run across the floor from the ballcarrier is very important. Remember: The receiver's stick should be held over his inside shoulder; that is, the stick is held behind the runner, not in front of him. By aiming slightly in front of the receiver's stick to a spot, the ball should arrive behind him when it makes contact with his stick.

- When running down the floor with a teammate on the opposite side of the floor, the rule is, it is better to throw the ball too far in front of the receiver rather than behind him. The receiver still may have a chance to catch the ball if it is still in front of him.

- A similar rule is employed when passing to a teammate on a breakaway: Over-pass rather than under-pass — throw a semi-lob, soft led pass to the receiver.

REMEMBER: When catching a breakaway pass, catch the ball over the inside shoulder. Place the stick with the face of the pocket parallel to the floor and in front and let the ball come to the pocket to avoid breaking stride.

• After catching a bad pass, remember to "pause for poise." This means, before a player makes the next pass, he should get everything together — balance, composure. By hurrying a return pass, a player often creates the chain reaction of yet another bad pass.

Photo 13: Catching a breakaway pass

— 5 —
Teaching Catching and Passing

To be successful, a team must be solid in fundamentals, especially in passing and catching.

Coaches must be aware that they have to fight boredom and lack of concentration in the players when teaching these skills. Also, most players think they already know how to pass and catch when they practice these fundamentals. So, it is important that the drills be fun, organized, competitive, short, varied, progressive, and game-like.

When teaching passing and catching, a coach must follow these principles:

- Assume that all players know nothing about passing and catching, and teach everything from the ground up.

- Have the players do the skill, rather than talk to them about how to do it.

- High repetition builds confidence.

- Have the drills favor success at the beginning.

- Concentrate on form first, accuracy second, and speed third.

- Follow this drill progression:

    1. Start the drills with both players stationary; then have one of the players running; then have both players running.

    2. Start with no pressure in the drill, then slowly create pressure by adding players (competition), adding time limits (race against the clock), or setting goals for the number of passes successfully completed.

- Make the losers of a competitive drill do token punishment.

- Have the passers call out the receiver's first name. This will help the players get into a habit of communicating on the floor.

- Have a criterion for the perfect pass: Expect a player to hit a receiver's stick, without the receiver having to move it, eight out of ten times at a distance three-quarters the width of the arena floor.

The Drills

A. Teach Holding a Stick First

Review the appropriate sections in chapters 1 and 2 on holding the stick. Gather your team into a semi-circle to review proper grips.

B. Teach Catching Second

Once the players have a good "grasp" of how to hold the stick, the first skill to work on is catching. Teaching the proper way to catch first saves a lot of wasted time running around picking up balls from passes missed through not knowing how to catch.

Another timesaver is, rather than having players attempt to throw the ball with their sticks before they know how, have the passers throw the ball with their hands to the receivers' sticks to start. This is a much more efficient way to teach catching, as most beginning players can throw the ball more accurately with their hands than with the lacrosse stick. Thus, the ball is more likely to end up near their partners' sticks where they can practice the skill of catching, rather than running after balls that have been badly thrown by a lacrosse stick.

For the following drills, put the players into two straight lines so that each is facing a partner.

1. Tennis Ball Throw

At first, have the passers throw tennis balls using their hands. Tennis balls are harder to catch because they are lighter than a regular lacrosse ball. Tennis balls create "soft hands" because players must "give" more with their sticks to help maintain the tennis ball in their sticks or the tennis balls will bounce out.

This exercise focuses on developing proper technique first, because the players don't have the weight of the lacrosse ball to tell them if they have caught it.

2. Lacrosse Ball Throw

Next, have the passers throw lacrosse balls with their hands. Tell the receivers to pretend, when the ball makes contact with the pocket, that the ball is an egg and they don't want to break it. This will emphasize the concept of "cushioning" the ball into the stick.

C. Teach Passing Third

1. Form Passing

Have players pass an imaginary ball so that you can observe and correct their technique. This allows the players to get the total picture of passing first.

2. Breakdown of the Fundamentals of Passing

Next, break down the fundamentals of passing. In this drill, try to isolate the different mechanics of passing.

a. Top Arm

First talk about the top arm's passing motion. This should be a swinging motion of the stick — straight back, straight forward. Some useful analogies here are "make a motion like you're casting a fishing rod," "make a motion like a Ferris wheel," or "pretend you're throwing a dart," to get the proper form of the top arm.

b. Wrist Movements

Next, get the players to throw with only wrist movement to stress the "snap" in the pass. Cock the wrists back and snap them forward. Cocking the wrists is a great power source.

Tell the players to hold both wrists as if they're going to box. Then have them cock their wrists backwards, then forwards. Doing this motion quickly will give the snapping motion desired.

c. Arm Movements

Get the players to throw with just the arms, stressing the extension of the top-hand arm and keeping the bottom-hand arm flexed. The top-hand arm provides the main power source by taking the stick straight back and bringing it straight forward.

d. Legs

The legs are another power source as the body weight is moved from the back foot to the forward foot.

e. Follow-through

On the follow-through of the stick after the release of the ball, make sure the tip of the stick ends up pointing at the target. For beginners, get them to exaggerate the follow-through by having them touch the floor with the head of their stick.

f. Putting It All Together

Finally, go back to the total picture by telling the players to make a motion like a Ferris wheel. Stress the snap of the wrists, full extension of the top-hand arm, good follow-through with the head of the stick, and stepping forward with the foot opposite to the stick. Again, get beginners to exaggerate the follow-through by having them touch the floor with the head of their stick.

3. Practicing with Darts

In their spare time, get the players to improve their passing technique and "touch" by throwing darts with their weak hand (their top-hand arm).

4. Individual Passing Drill to the Same Receiver

Another good progression to teach strictly passing is to line up 4–5 players with a ball in a straight line. Each player passes to a coach or a good player who can catch the ball. Each player in the line takes a turn at passing the ball to the receiver. The passer then goes to the end of the line, while the receiver catches the ball and rolls it back to the next passer in line. Then the next passer passes, and so on.

You need a good receiver for this drill because, even though they'll be trying to hit the target, the inexperienced passers are going to end up passing the ball all over the place. A good receiver should still be able to catch the wayward ball and roll it back to the next person in line.

D. Individual Passing Drill: Passing Against a Wall

Passing against the wall is the oldest drill in any shooting or throwing sport, but this simple drill makes great players and great shooters. Going to a wall or an arena and throwing a ball for a couple of hours takes self-discipline, a burning desire to be great, and a great love of the game.

For lacrosse players, passing against a wall allows them to concentrate on just the swinging motion of the stick rather than the target. Once players start to develop the proper "feeling" of passing, they can then concentrate on hitting the target.

The height of the target on the wall is important. Players should be using two types of targets: one should be as high as they would want to throw a ball to a receiver's stick; the other target should be the shape of a lacrosse net where they can pick the top corners and bottom corners.

E. Pair Passing Drills

1. Stationary Passing with One Ball

Put all players in two straight lines, with each opposite a partner.

a.   Two players pass the ball back and forth. Concentrate on technique and accuracy.

   i)   Start the drill with the players facing each other until they get the proper overhand technique. Stress to the players that they should not bring their sticks across their bodies on the follow-through, but should follow through straight ahead with the top arm extended.

   ii)   Once the players throw with a perfect overhand technique, have them turn their bodies sideways to the receivers. This is the more natural stance taken in a game when they have the ball, where the chances of their being cross-checked or harassed are very great. This stance puts them in a better position to protect their stick and still pass.

b.   To put pressure on the players:

- Keep track of how many catches the partners can make without dropping the ball.
- Keep track of the number of catches made in 30 seconds.
- Acknowledge the pair that catches 20 passes first.

Start the drill with all the balls on one side of the floor and as the players catch the ball, they both call out the number of catches made. At the beginning of the drill, the partners can compete against themselves by improving against their last count; then, as the team gets better, the partners can compete against each other.

c.   Have the passers throw all the passes to their partner's off-stick side. This drill will help players become comfortable catching the ball on the wrong side of their body.

d.   Again, use tennis balls to pass back and forth to help the players work on the proper mechanics of passing and catching and to create "soft hands."

2. Stationary Passing with Two Balls

In this drill both players must throw overhand passes concentrating on catching one ball while making a good pass with the other. The coach should make this a game to see which partners can keep the balls going the longest without dropping them.

Variation: One partner throws an overhand pass while the other partner throws a bounce pass; when the coach yells "Change!" the partners switch to the other type of pass.

3. Stationary Pair Passing with Defensive Pressure

Another name for this drill is "Monkey in the Middle." The partners stand about 15 feet (4.5 metres) apart. The defender standing in the middle attacks the ballcarrier, trying to force a bad pass while attempting to get his stick in the way of the pass.

The defender cannot cross-check, but can interfere with the passer's stick in any way. If the defender touches the ball or forces a bad pass, he switches position with the passer on whom he forced the bad pass.

Passes cannot be lobbed over the defender's head, but must be level. The passer must pass around the defender's stick while staying in a small area.

Note   *The fake pass really helps to relieve pressure in this drill.*

Variation: In a real game, beginning players try to make passes while being checked, with the result that the ball is turned over. Use a variation of the drill above except that the passers have more room to move around. This teaches players not to panic when being harassed by defenders, but to relax and get in the clear with speed and intelligence. One way to get away from pressure is to fake a step in one direction, then step in the other direction; another way is to attack the defender, then back off from the pressure and throw the ball around his stick.

The important point to stress with this drill is not to take a hit or be interfered with when making a pass.

4. Partners Passing on the Run

Before describing this next drill, a review of some terms in case you are not familiar with them: In lacrosse a player who naturally holds his stick over his left shoulder is usually called a "left-hand shot" or "left shot." A left-hand shot plays on the right side of the floor, while facing the opposition net, so that his stick faces into the middle of the floor. Right-hand shots — right shots — do the same on the left side of the floor.

This positioning of players according to how they shoot is done for two reasons: to get a better angle shot at the net and, while taking a cross-check, to take a hit and still get a good shot off.

Now to the drill. Make a line of right shots and a line of left shots at one end of the floor. Partners (a right and a left shot) will run to the other end of the floor, passing the ball back and forth, then waiting when they reach the end. As soon as the first set of partners leaves, the next pair goes, and so on.

This is strictly a passing drill and therefore no shots are taken. To ensure there are lots of passes on the way down the floor, state this rule: "Players cannot take more than two steps with the ball without passing it." Stress calling out the receiver's name and keeping the stick up for a good target.

Variation: Run the partners narrow or wide according to the positioning they are imitating. A narrow width would be as wide as the crease around the net; a wide distance would be from one side face-off circle to the opposite side face-off circle.

F. Group Passing Drills

1. Knock Out Drill

In this drill, there are six players and two balls. Three players line up opposite the other three. Players pass the balls back and forth as quickly as they can. The only rule is that a player can't throw to another player who has a ball in his stick.

Players who drop a pass or passers who throw a bad pass that the receiver can't catch get a demerit point. If they hit five demerit points, they must drop out of the drill.

The drill ends with two players and two balls. Eventually, one player with the lowest number of demerit points becomes the winner *(see Diagram 1 below)*.

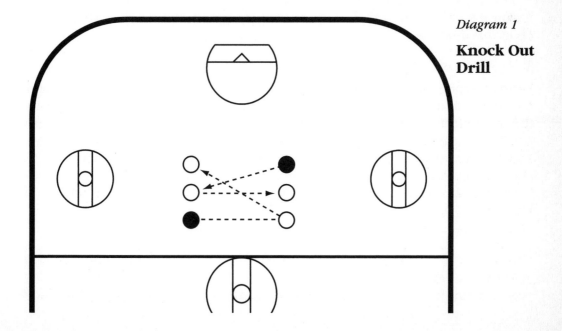

Diagram 1

Knock Out Drill

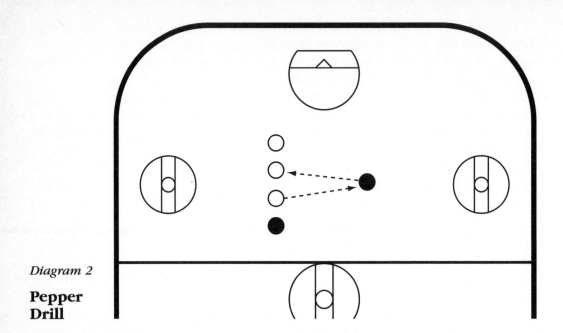

Diagram 2

**Pepper
Drill**

2. Pepper Drill

Set up this drill with one player facing four others who are in a straight line. Using two balls, the group passes the balls back and forth to the individual passer.

The objective of the drill is to make the lone passer work as hard as possible on his ballhandling skills. Stress accuracy, speed, and quick releases. *(See Diagram 2 above.)*

3. Zig-Zag Drill

Form two long lines facing each other, and put a full bucket of balls at one end of the line and an empty bucket at the other end. The drill can be run with the whole team or with lines (groups of five).

Players pass the balls down the lines in a zig-zag fashion. The players have no pressure on them, giving them time to work on their technique and accuracy. This drill also gives coaches lots of time to walk around and give feedback to all the players while they are all involved in passing and catching. *(See Diagram 3, opposite.)*

The next six variations of the zig-zag drill help to put pressure on the players to make them concentrate more.

a. Pressure through Punishment

Players who drop a good pass or throw a bad one must do five pushups for every dropped ball. Players stay in the drill and do their pushups after all the balls have been sent down the line.

b. Pressure through an Objective

Set an objective such as the following: Out of 20 balls thrown down the line, at least 14 must end up in the bucket at the other end. The drill must not be stopped until the objective is met, so be sure the objective is realistic and obtainable.

c. Pressure through Number of Times

Players count the number of times they can pass one ball down and back the line without dropping it. After they have done it once, they have a standard they try to beat the next time. A variation is to set a predetermined objective of the number of times players can pass the ball down and back without dropping it.

d. Pressure through Time

Using a stop watch, the coach times how long it takes a ball to go down and back without being dropped. Again, the team is always trying to beat its best time.

e. Pressure through Competition

Keeping the same type of formation, put the players in their "lines" of groups of five. The lines compete against each other to see who can keep the ball going the longest without dropping it, or who can pass the ball the quickest down and back three times.

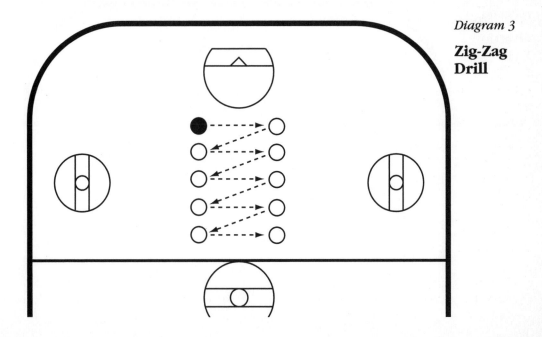

Diagram 3

**Zig-Zag
Drill**

f. Pressure through Movement

Put six to eight players in a zig-zag formation with the rest of the team at one end — everyone with a ball.

The first ballcarrier passes the ball to the first player and follows his pass to the first player's position; the first player then passes to his teammate opposite him and also follows his pass.

The players continue this replace-the-receiver procedure all the way down the line; the player at the end of the zig-zag line runs back to the end of the straight line with the ball.

The drill is over when everybody has returned to his original spot. Time the drill to see if the team can beat their previous best time.

4. Shuttle Drill

Form two lines: One group of three players lines up behind each other, facing another group of two players lined up behind each other. Using one ball, the ballcarrier will pass to the opposite line and run behind the receiver's line; the receiver then passes back to the other line and runs behind it; this procedure continues until the end of the drill.

Stress that players concentrate on the target, give horizontal passes or "passing" passes, and keep the ball in the air — as soon as the ball hits their stick they are throwing it.

Work on short passes — the width of the floor — or long passes — the length of the floor. Put pressure into the drill by counting the number of pass-

Diagram 4

Shuttle Drill

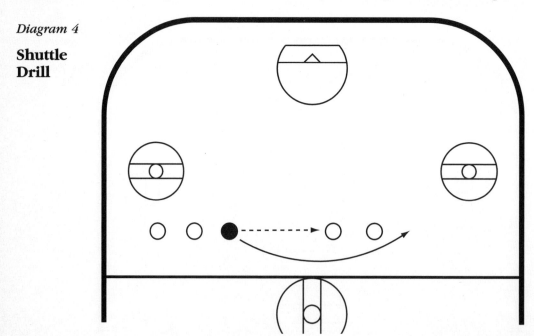

es in 30 seconds, or by having the "lines" compete against each other to see which line can keep the ball in the air the longest without dropping it. *(See Diagram 4, opposite.)*

5. Single Line Drill

Use six stationary passers, three on each side of the floor spaced out along the boards — one player above the side face-off circle, one at center along the boards, and the third before the far side face-off circle. All the left shots with a ball line up on one side of the floor and all the rights with a ball line up on the other side. The players naturally line up on their proper side.

The first right shot passes to the opposite stationary passer and sprints down the floor looking for a return pass. He then passes to the next stationary passer and looks for the return pass, and does the same thing to the last passer. This is a no-shot drill. When the runner has caught the ball from the last passer, he runs behind the net, lining up to come back the other way.

Once right shot leaves, the first left-shot player executes the same procedure. The lines alternate until everybody has practiced the give-and-go technique down the floor. *(See Diagram 5 below.)*

Variation: The players can take a shot at both ends of the floor. Make a game of left shots versus right shots. The winning team is the one that scores the most goals down and back. Also, run the drill for five minutes, keeping the stats on how many passes are completed, or on how many shots are taken and how many are scored by the whole team.

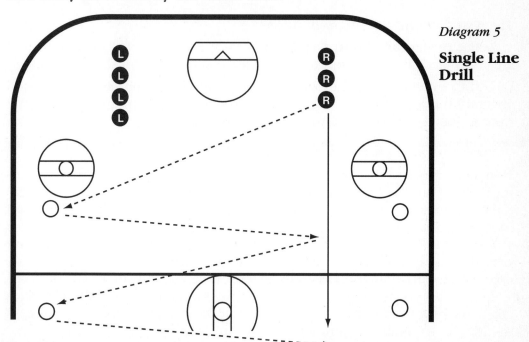

Diagram 5

Single Line Drill

6. Three-on-Two Pressure Passing

Three stationary players in the half-floor area pass the ball around, quickly trying to score. The two defenders and the goalie do anything to stop them from scoring. The best opportunity to score is after one or two quick passes.

7. Five-on-Five Keep Away

Play 5-on-5, with the line that makes the highest number of passes the winners. Usually this is played in the half-floor area. The coach counts the number of passes made (no shots). If the defensive team forces a bad pass or forces the ball to hit the floor, the team that dropped the ball loses possession to its opposition.

8. Borden Ball

Play 5-on-5 full floor. The game has three rules:

• a player must pass the ball in three seconds;

• a player can only take three steps with the ball before he must pass it; and

• if a team drops the ball, it loses possession.

Any violation of the rules puts the ball over to the other team. Teams can play for a certain length of time or until one team scores a certain number of goals. Stress that players must work to get open for the pass; they must move and not stand still; and the ballcarrier must see the whole floor.

The next few drills use these positions:

Left Creaseman, Right Creaseman — these are forward positions and are often placed near the opposition's crease at the front of the fast-break.

Left Cornerman, Right Cornerman — these positions are often placed about 15 feet (4.5 metres) behind the creasemen; they bring the ball up the floor in the fast-break and usually initiate the team offense.

9. Four Corner Fast-Break Passing Drill

Four players stand in the two creasemen's positions and the two cornermen's positions. The players "tic-tac-toe" the ball around as quickly and accurately as possible. The players should be urged not to make the same pass twice in a row. *(See Diagram 6, opposite.)*

Variation: The ballcarrier pretends he is being pressured by a rushing defender and backs off so he does not take a hit while passing. The new ballcarrier now backs off and passes to another receiver, and so on.

In a 4-on-3 situation, one of the major rules is that the ballcarrier cannot take a hit by a defender. (A hit will force the ballcarrier to throw a bad pass resulting in a possible turnover.)

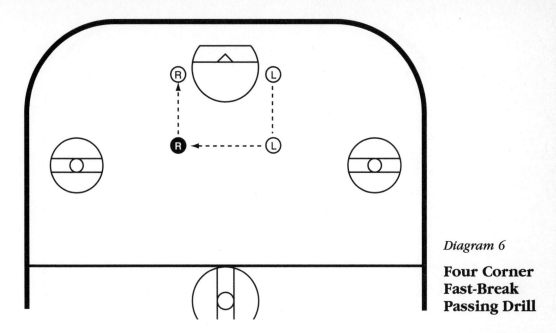

Diagram 6

Four Corner Fast-Break Passing Drill

So to counter a defender attacking the ballcarrier, the ballcarrier must back off or backpedal to pass the ball without taking a hit.

10. Four Corner Offense Passing Drill

a. V-Cut Drill

This drill teaches the concept of getting in the clear. Players in the cornerman's position must do a "down and back" V-cut before receiving a cross-floor pass from the ballcarrier in the other cornerman's position. This move stops the defender from intercepting the dangerous cross-floor pass and breaking down the floor.

The receiver must fake a cut through the middle by looking at the ballcarrier as if he is going to receive a pass. Then suddenly he must stop, push off with his outside foot, and return to wherever he came from to receive the pass. He must make sure his stick is extended fully to give the passer a good target and the receiver that extra edge so that the pass is not intercepted.

Players in the cornerman's position must also do a "down and back" V-cut before receiving a pass from the ballcarrier in the creaseman's position. The player still fakes a cut and looks at the ballcarrier but stops on his inside foot and pushes off, backpedaling to the spot he left, giving his stick target inside his body, which is the most natural position.

Players in the creaseman's position must do an "in and out" V-cut before receiving a pass into the corner area of the floor from the ballcarrier in the cornerman's position on his side of the floor. It's best to receive the pass as close

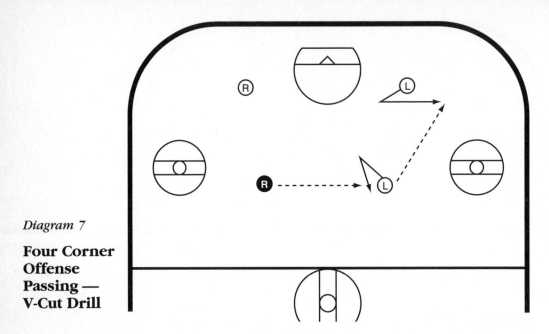

Diagram 7

Four Corner Offense Passing — V-Cut Drill

to the net as possible to be an instant threat with the ball. To accomplish this, he must fake a cut to the net to draw the defender, then stop suddenly on his inside foot, and break out to a scoring position or farther. Extend the stick to give a good target and to give the receiver an edge to prevent an interception.

The four players pass the ball around the outside, making these moves over and over again with no shots. *(See Diagram 7 above.)*

b. Interchange (Exchange) Drill (See Diagram 8, opposite)

This drill helps players to move on offense and gives them another option for throwing the cross-floor pass without the worry of an interception.

Here, the off-ball players just exchange positions from the cornerman's position to the creaseman's position and vice versa while the ballcarrier throws a cross-floor pass from the cornerman's position.

Once the ballcarrier throws the cross-floor pass, he then runs to interchange with his teammate, who should be in the clear for the next cross-floor pass. Timing is important: the ballcarrier must let the off-ball side develop.

The players just keep running the drill over and over again. There is no shot on goal. The player leaving the crease position cuts on the outside of his teammate while the player coming down on the exchange cuts on the inside of his teammate. The reason for this movement is that the player coming down may run into his teammate's opponent, thereby putting his teammate in the clear.

c. "Down Pick" Drill

This drill is similar to (b), the Interchange Drill. It is a continuous-movement

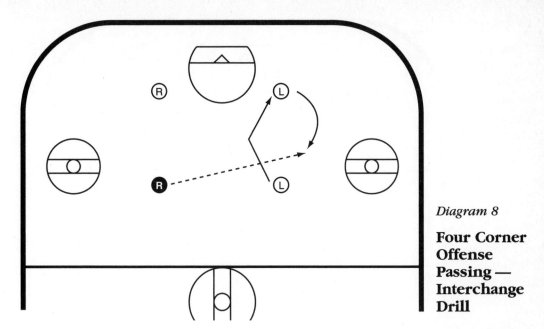

Diagram 8

Four Corner Offense Passing — Interchange Drill

drill with no shot on goal. The picker (the player who sets a pick on his team-mate's defender) runs a V-formation on the off-ball side when setting the down pick on the imaginary defender. Players keep setting down picks and throwing cross-floor passes. *(See Diagram 9, next page.)*

d. Cut and Replace Drill

This is a good drill to get players into the habit of passing and cutting. It is a continuous-movement drill, with no shot on goal.

The ballcarrier in the cornerman's position throws a cross-floor pass, then cuts into the middle looking for a return pass. Once he gets to the middle, he stays on his own side and replaces the creaseman who has just replaced the cornerman's position. Just as the creaseman replaces the cornerman's position he should be receiving the next cross-floor pass. *(See Diagram 10, next page.)*

e. Four-on-Four Pressure Passing

This is still a passing drill, but with defensive pressure. The players run the drill continually moving and passing, with the offensive players now being covered by defenders.

11. Four Corner "Follow Your Pass" Drill

The players stand in a box formation, about the distance they would have in a game, with the players divided up evenly at each corner. They pass one ball in one direction, and follow their pass, going to the back of the line they passed to.

Diagram 9

**Four
Corner
Offense
Passing —
Down Pick
Drill**

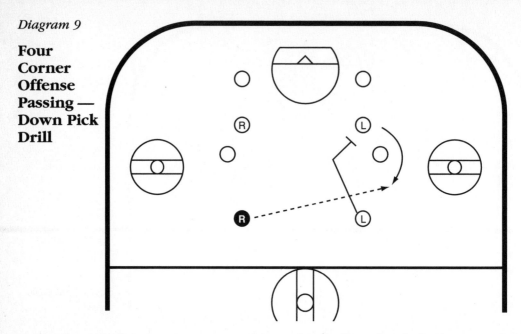

As their proficiency improves, add another ball to the drill. Now, two balls are being passed in the same direction, so the second player in each line has to stay alert for a pass. Then, progress to three balls and possibly four.

In this drill the players must concentrate on communication (remember, passers call out the receiver's name in our passing drills); precision passing and catching; and knowing whether they are passing in clockwise or counter-clockwise direction, because when the coach calls "Change," the players change their passing direction.

Diagram 10

**Four
Corner
Offense
Passing —
Cut and
Replace
Drill**

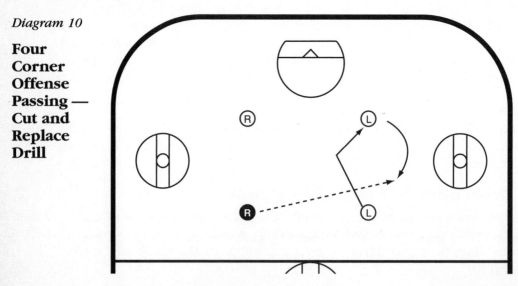

— 6 —
Loose Ball Strategies

Usually, the team that can control loose balls wins the game. Fighting for loose balls is one of the hardest things to do in any game, because it involves effort, physical contact, composure, and technique.

I. Scoop Pick-up Technique

Players should practice only the scoop pick-up method for picking up all types of loose balls. The scoop is used when picking up a rolling or bouncing ball. There are other types of pick-ups but they aren't as effective; there is the "Indian" pick-up (too fancy) and the "trap & scoop" (takes too long).

Focus on the following when practicing the scoop pick-up method:

- Keep the eyes on the ball.
- Bend the knees to get low. A player closer to the floor has a lower center of gravity. This helps him to maintain better balance, which will help him to scoop up the rolling ball more easily.
- Grab the stick at its throat with the top hand. This forces the player to bend over more to get closer to the floor and helps him to concentrate on the loose ball.
- Keep the bottom hand low to the floor so the stick is almost parallel to the floor. The player can then scoop the rolling ball into his stick using a "shoveling" motion. Remember: Scoop "through" the ball.
- Always keep two hands on the stick when fighting for a loose ball, and for control once the ball is in the stick.
- The foot opposite the stick side should be planted close to the ball for better balance.

Photos 14 & 15: Scoop pick-up rolling ball, and cradle

- Approach a loose ball on the stick side if there is no defensive pressure, because it is quicker to scoop the ball up on the run with the stick on that side of the body.

- When fighting for a loose ball, the player should try to get his body between the opponent and the ball. A player usually picks up the ball in front of his body (rather than the side of his body), whether the ball is lying on the floor or bouncing. So he has to hold his stick slightly to the side and in front of his body when scooping up the ball, using his body to shield his stick.

- On possession of the ball, the player should slide his top hand up the shaft to the throat of the stick if it is not already there, to cradle the ball and to protect the stick with his body.

II. Loose Ball Tips

- Obtaining a loose ball is 75% desire and 25% ability and technique.
- A good loose-ball player must have an aggressive, mentally tough atti-

tude, knowing he is going to be hit or checked on all loose balls. He cannot be afraid to go after a loose ball.

- When going after a loose ball, a player has to believe he is going to be in a war for possession of the ball. So, he must be aggressive and attack every loose ball like it belongs to him. Remember: Players should never stand and wait for a ball to come to them. They must attack every loose ball and firmly believe that every loose ball is theirs. They must be persistent and determined, with an attitude of never giving up.

- Because of the importance of loose balls, two players should go after every one.

- Contest every loose ball. Never concede it to the opposition, because every loose ball is a chance to score.

- If the opposition gets possession of the ball, continue to pressure the ballcarrier so he cannot pass the ball down the floor to his teammates. This is strictly a delaying tactic, not a stealing tactic.

Note *If a player tries to steal the ball off the ballcarrier by stick-checking, he usually gets beaten.*

Photo 16:
Scoop pick-up,
bouncing ball

Photos 17 & 18: Stepping in front of an opponent while fighting for the loose ball.

- When going into the boards with an opponent, a player should remember the following:

  1. If the player goes in first, he should use his body to protect the ball before he actually tries to pick it up. He should be ready to lean back into his check and brace himself in case his opponent plans to cross-check him from behind. On possession of the ball, he must cradle and protect it immediately. Stress keeping the stick close to the body, in a vertical position, and maintaining the body between the stick and the opponent.

  2. If the opponent goes in first, the player should play his opponent's stick to stop him from picking up the ball. He should never stand back and let an opponent just pick up the ball. The player should avoid cross-checking from behind; this type of move reveals a player's selfishness, laziness and stupidity — on any hit from behind the offensive player will be awarded possession of the ball, or the hitter will be awarded a two-minute penalty, or a major penalty depending on the severity of the hit.

Note   *The most important aspect of going after a loose ball is assuming that the opponent, if he's first, is going to miss or mishandle the ball.*

3. When a player gains possession of the ball and knows he is going to get hit along the boards, he should keep moving, absorbing the check by leaning into it, and making sure he instigates the hit.

• Once a player has control of the ball, he has three options:

1. Pass the ball up the floor quickly to take advantage of any lapse by the opposition defense.

2. Run the ball up the floor.

3. Pass the ball back to a teammate or goalie if he gets into trouble. This pass has to be an emergency because it goes against one of the main Fast-Break principles: A player should never pass back.

III. Loose Ball Drills

These are "attitude" drills to instill aggressiveness, persistence, and determination. These drills are done regularly, but can be done more often if the team was not aggressive and hungry for loose balls during their last game.

While doing these drills, coaches should emphasize the following to the players:

• Have a "never say die" attitude.

• Attack all loose balls.

• Getting loose balls takes courage and heart.

Use this drill progression in regards to the speed of the ball:

1. Start with a stationary ball and let the players "run through" the ball. "Run through" means the player doesn't slow down to pick up the ball, but maintains his same speed while picking up the ball.

2. Players work on picking up a slow bouncing ball going away from them, either straight ahead or at an angle, and then on balls bouncing towards them. Eventually increase the speed of the ball so that it is moving quickly away from the players, then coming towards them.

3. Players then work on the much harder routine of picking up a fast-rolling ball, in the same progression as in "**2**" above.

Drill progression in regards to defensive pressure:

1. Start with no defensive pressure until the players are able to pick up the ball properly.

2. Then add some token defensive pressure to the drills. For example, start the defender behind the offensive player to give the offensive player an advantage.

3. Finally, run a live drill where there will be defensive pressure.

1. Individual Practice

A player shoots the ball off an outside wall and lets it roll along the grass. When the ball hits the grass it will do crazy bounces and hops. The player then has to attack and react to the ball.

It is harder to retrieve a ball coming off a rough surface such as grass or gravel than off a cement floor or artificial turf. This drill will help a player react quickly to loose balls in a game.

2. Stationary Pick-up Drill

Players line up in groups of six. In front of them is one coach with a bucket of balls. The coach places a ball on the ground and the first player runs and picks up the stationary ball. Another coach will give feedback on the player's scoop technique.

3. Partners "Attack" Drill

Each partner faces the other standing near their side boards. One partner rolls the ball across the floor towards the other, who scoops it up while attacking the ball coming at him. The ballcarrier then runs back to his original spot and rolls it towards his partner, who is now running at him.

4. Partners "Chase" Drill

Partners stand side-by-side near the side boards. One partner rolls the ball away from his partner, who chases the rolling ball and scoops it up. Then the partners switch roles.

5. Loose Ball Zig-Zag Drill

Use the same formation as the Passing Zig-Zag Drill (p. 48). Players starting at one end will roll or bounce the ball down the line in a zig-zag pattern.

6. Loose Ball Shuttle Drill

Use the same formation as the Passing Shuttle Drill (p. 50). Players starting at one line will roll or bounce the ball to the opposite line and run behind the receiver's line. This is a good drill because players learn to attack the ball.

7. Loose Ball Single Line Drill

Use the same set-up as in the Passing Single Line Drill (p. 51), with six sta-tionary passers, three on each side of the floor. Lefts and rights line up on their proper side of the floor at one end, everybody having a ball. The first left shot passes the ball to the first stationary passer opposite him, who in turn rolls the ball in front of the runner, who picks up the loose ball and then passes to the next player.

8. "Rebounds Off the Boards" Drill

Five players form a single line facing the boards about 15 feet (4.5 metres) away.

The first player with a ball will bang it off the boards. Then the next player in line attacks the ball, but only after it hits the boards, and not before. After this player bangs the ball off the boards, he goes back to the end of the line.

The coach can control the type of bounce he wants coming off the boards. He can tell the players to bang the ball off the boards low so it will roll along the floor, or to bang the ball off the boards higher so there is a higher bounce.

Stress that players should charge the ball with all-out intensity.

9. Partners "Rebound off the Boards" Drill

One player faces the boards from about six feet (two metres) out. The other throws the ball off the boards. His partner reacts to the rebound, picks it up, and passes it back to the first player.

Variation: Partners face each other and the rebounder does not turn to retrieve the ball until it hits the boards.

10. "Courage in the Corner" Drills

a. One-on-One Blocking Out Drill

This drill helps players learn to protect the ball with their bodies. The ball and the two players are along the side boards.

The defensive player starts immediately behind the offensive player. On the whistle, the offensive player moves around to ward off the defensive player, who is trying to pick up the ball. The offensive player protects the ball and does not try to pick it up.

Players should keep their eye on the ball, stay low, and maintain a wide stance.

b. Token Defense Drill

Two lines of players are lined up about 20 feet (6 metres) from the corner. The coach designates one line offensive and the other defensive. The coach then rolls the ball into the corner or places the ball in the corner.

On the whistle, the first two players in the front of each line fight for the ball in the corner. Both players attack the ball, with the designated defensive player using "token" defense so that the offense can work on protecting the ball with his body while picking up the ball. The defender is not allowed to pick up the ball. The coach can set this up by starting the defender one step behind the offensive player.

Points to stress in this drill:

- Once they have possession, players should pull the stick in close to the body and cradle it.

- Players should always anticipate a hit upon picking up a loose ball. They should avoid exposing the front of their body to the action by keeping their body turned sideways in case of a possible cross-check by the defender.

c. "Courage in the Corner" Game

The coach picks two teams by pairing players by weight and quickness. The first two players from each team will battle for the loose ball in the corner.

The coach will roll the ball into the corner. The players will go on the whistle or when the ball hits the boards. A player gets one point for his team for possession. The first team to reach 10 points is the winner; losers do 10 pushups. *(See Diagram 11.)*

Variation 1: The player who gets the ball tries to score and the other play-

Diagram 11

"Courage in the Corner" game

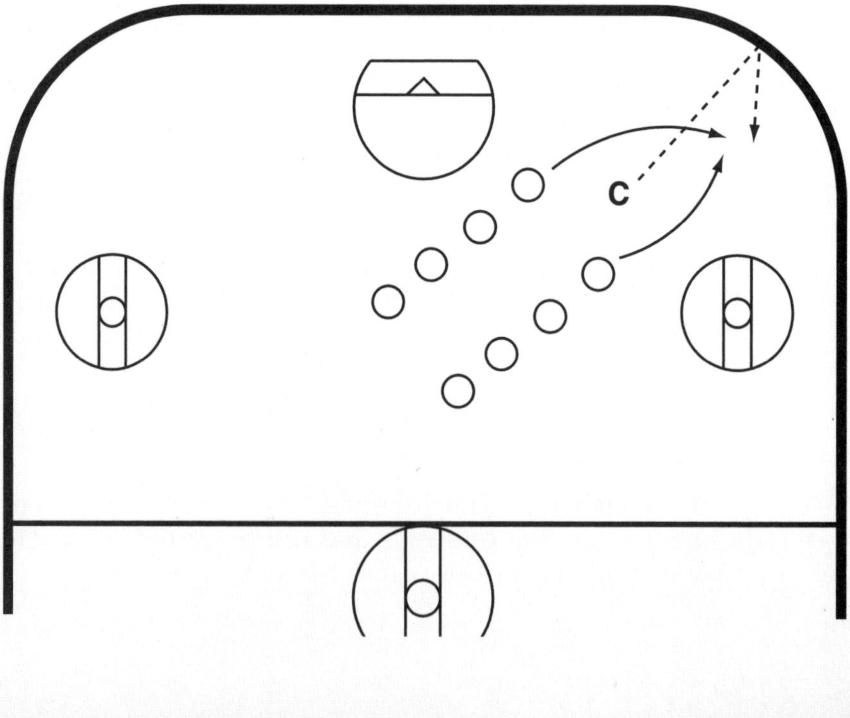

er tries to stop him. The ballcarrier gets a point for possession and another point if he scores.

Variation 2: The player gets possession in the corner and passes out to a passer, then breaks to the net for a return pass, trying to score. A player gets a point for possession, a point for receiving a return pass, and a point for a score.

Variation 3: Coach designates one line offensive and the other defensive. If the offensive player gets the ball, he tries to score; if the defensive player gets it, he tries to run the ball up to center against defensive pressure in five seconds.

Both players get a point for possession; the offensive player receives an additional point if he scores; the defensive player receives an additional point if he gets the ball to center within five seconds.

Variation 4: This variation is called "War" and is played at the end of practice. Players pair up; the player who gets possession of the loose ball goes to the showers early, while his partner stays to battle another teammate for possession.

11. "Courage Along the Board" Drill

Similar to the previous drill, players go through a series of progressions.

a. "Lean into Check" Drill

All players are with partners along the boards. The offensive player practices picking up a ball with token defensive pressure. The checker just leans on the offensive player's body with his stick. The offensive player leans into the checker with his back or sideways with his arm as he picks up the ball.

b. "Push Check" Drill

The defensive player now pushes on the offensive player's body. The offensive player absorbs the checks by leaning slightly in the direction of the hits and relaxing.

c. "Stick Check" Drill

The defensive player is restricted only to playing the offensive player's stick as he tries to pick up the ball.

> **Note**　*Stick-checking involves the defensive player trying to jar the ball loose from the offense player by hitting the offensive player's stick with his stick.*

d. "Courage Along the Boards" Game

This is similar to the "Courage in the Corner" game described above, except the two opposing players fight for the ball along the boards.

12. "Courage in the Middle" Game

This is similar to the other "Courage" games above. The coach stands in the middle of the floor between the two teams and rolls the ball into the open floor. The first two players battle for the loose ball, then go one-on-one.

Variation: Players battle for a stationary ball.

13. Two-on-Two "Courage in the Corner" Drill

The same as the "Courage in the Corner" drill (no. 10), but with two players from each line battling each other for the ball.

14. Two-on-One "Courage in the Corner" Drill

Designate one offensive player and two defensive players. The first defensive teammate takes the offensive player, while the second teammate picks up the ball.

15. "Animal" Drill

Put the players in groups of four. Three players fight for the loose ball in the corner. The first player who gets two loose balls sits out, while the next player comes in the drill. Then the three players start the drill all over again. Stress no hitting from behind!

Variation: The player who gets the ball tries to score while the other two players try to stop him. If the ballcarrier scores, he is out of the drill.

16. "Get It" Game

Put four balls on the floor. Five players try to get them. The loser does sprints.

17. "Battle" Drill

This is a five-on-five loose ball drill. Throw the ball in the middle of two teams. The winner is whoever gets the ball.

— 7 —
Individual Offense (One-on-One Moves)

THE QUALITIES of a great one-one-one player are quickness, balance, power, intelligence and deception. Great one-on-one players have a great knack of beating people. They do it naturally or automatically without even thinking of what they are doing.

One-on-one moves are generally broken into two types:

Strong-Side Move — This move is used when an offensive player goes one-on-one and cuts into the middle of the floor. The strong-side move is made frequently, because it is the most natural move — the stick is held facing the middle of the floor, giving the player the best scoring opportunity.

Counter Move — This move wasn't that common a few years ago but now is as popular as the strong-side move. With this move the ballcarrier cuts to the outside of the floor. By cutting to the boards, the ballcarrier must eventually come back inside to get into a good scoring position. Most players use the counter move in case they are being overplayed from going into the middle, or just as a change in their repertoire.

I. One-On-One Techniques

All the techniques in this section refer to left-handed shots.

A. Physically Beating a Defender

1. Inside Slide Move (Taking a Hit — See Photo 19)

This is the most difficult — but also the most common and most effective — of all one-on-one moves.

a. In this strong-side move, a ballcarrier's first priority is to protect his stick. He does this by turning his body sideways to take the cross-check on the upper arm of his non-stick side, thereby using his body as a shield for his stick.

b. Before the check, a ballcarrier should choke up on his stick, i.e., move his top hand up close to the throat of the stick. This gives the ballcarrier better control for cradling when taking heavy cross-checking.

c. A ballcarrier should hold his stick vertically, while executing the large cradle (see p. 24) on contact, instead of holding his stick horizontally. Holding the stick horizontally makes it easier to be stick-checked, and there is also a higher probability of the ball falling out on the jar of the hit.

    Most players hold the stick vertically in close to the body, but some like to hold the stick vertically away from the body, two arms fully extended; this is just a personal preference.

d. A ballcarrier should watch the checker over his shoulder rather than watching the ball in his stick.

e. A ballcarrier also has to learn to lean into the check and to relax on the impact of the cross-check, instead of tightening up and possibly coughing up the ball on a jarring hit.

f. On contact, a ballcarrier should have a solid base i.e., feet spread wider than shoulder-width apart to maintain balance. On receiving a cross-

Photo 19: Inside Slide Move — large cradle, wide stance, look over your shoulder.

check, some of the bigger ballcarriers like to use their asset, their size, by initiating the contact with their upper arm and body weight to see if the defender is good enough to stop him.

g. The ballcarrier's objective is to try to make contact at the "head" area of the stick or off-center of the defender's stick so he can slide off his check, beating his opponent for a good shot on net. The ballcarrier can also try to hit the stick at an angle rather than dead on, making it easier to slide past the defender. By leaning into his check's stick with his body weight and keeping a wide stance, the ballcarrier will keep good balance.

h. After beating the defender, the ballcarrier should remember to tuck the stick in front of his body and keep it in this vertical position to protect it until he is ready to shoot.

Or, if the ballcarrier just keeps cutting across the top, he can lean into his check to equalize pressure and shoot around his defender.

Or, the ballcarrier can lean into the cross-checks, and try to pick up his defender's cross-checking rhythm. Then, as the defender commits, the ballcarrier steps away from his opponent so that the latter either reaches for air and becomes off balance, making it easier for the ballcarrier to go around him, or makes contact at the end of his hit and ends up merely pushing the ballcarrier forward rather than stopping him.

2. Outside Slide Move

This is a counter to the Inside Slide Move. The ballcarrier turns his body sideways facing the boards, and taking the cross-check on his stick-side upper arm. At the same time as he turns his body, he swings his stick outside, holding it with two hands and in close to the body to protect the stick with his body. The ballcarrier must he ready for an over-the-head check or defender trying to reach around his to stick check him.

The ballcarrier now tries to slide past the defender on the outside and then cut back inside of the defender. The battle is for the ballcarrier to get his body in front of the defender.

If the ballcarrier trying to get back in front of the defender moves out of scoring territory, i.e., too close to the corner area, he must have a counter move, which is the Roll Move. If the defender cuts off the ballcarrier, he spins back across the top.

3. Roll Move

a. Use the same positioning as in the Inside Slide Move (p. 67), except this time the ballcarrier puts his back into the defender, then rolls back and forth or from side to side, trying to get the defender to commit to cutting him off in the direction he is rolling. Once the defender commits, the ballcarrier rolls back the other way, going to the net.

b. In this rolling position, use the upper body, lean a bit more with the body weight, keep the feet moving, and use deception to beat the defender.

Variation: When cutting across the top while being cross-checked, the ballcarrier fakes a half-roll to the outside, putting his back on the defender's stick. Then, when the defender commits by trying to stop this half-roll, he continues back across the top for a shot or a move to the net.

4. Bull Move

a. This power move relies on the ability to go in and overpower the defender when the ballcarrier is stronger and bigger. Remember: Move the top hand up the shaft to cradle the ball better and tighten the arm and body on the instant of contact, because in this situation the ballcarrier is initiating the contact.

b. The ballcarrier drives through the defender's stick, trying to knock him off-balance or just run right over him.

Variation: The ballcarrier can run through the hit, push the defender back, while at the same time backing off, creating a gap for a shot or a fake shot.

5. Bait Move

While being cross-checked, the ballcarrier fools his defensive man by exposing his stick over his shoulder, creating such a temptation for the checker that he cannot resist going after it. As the defender commits, the ballcarrier quickly pulls his stick around in front of his body, ending up in front of his defender and going to the net.

B. General Fake Technique

1. The Fake

This is a move of lateral quickness with little or no contact while facing the defender. The ballcarrier initiates an action to get a reaction from the defender. The "fake" move is to make the defender move in one direction while the ballcarrier goes in the other.

It is important to make the fake step look convincing; it must look like the real thing. All the ballcarrier needs to do is to get his opponent leaning in one direction and therefore off-balance or committing himself to the fake step by reacting to the move. Then the ballcarrier takes a quick step in the other direction.

Note   *If player is running "north," he steps "east or west" and
then continues in a "northerly direction.*

Although the fake entails a change of direction, the change should only be
slight — one–two steps in either direction. The ballcarrier runs straight at the
defender and beats him in a confined area while continuing to maintain the
path of a straight line. The fake should not have the ballcarrier running wide,
as this could possibly give the defender time to recover.

2. Movement of the Defender

The success in beating an opponent lies in "moving the defender." If both players are standing still and the offensive player makes a move, the defender can
still react quickly to stay with him. But if the ballcarrier is walking or jogging,
the defender will be moving backwards or moving alongside him; then, when
the offensive player suddenly fakes and cuts sharply (changes direction), the
defender has to fight the lag of his physical reaction time to stay with him —
the defender will have difficulty making a quick change of direction when he
has already committed to another direction.

Also, the defender having to overcome his momentum from one direction
to another might unbalance himself, while the ballcarrier will be balanced
and controlled. This will give the ballcarrier the half-step needed to beat the
opponent.

3. Footwork

A ballcarrier beats his man with his feet rather than faking with his head (bob-
bing) or moving his body around.

To set the defensive man up, the ballcarrier works on the "jab" step: He
plants his foot as if going in a certain direction — to look believable, the "fake"
step has to be convincing. Then, pushing off the faking foot, he takes an explosive step with his other foot in the opposite direction (V-cut).

So, when a ballcarrier wants to go one way, he will take a fake step before
he goes there, or take the defender two or three steps in the opposite direction and then make his move. Again, the important thing is to get the defender moving so he will be vulnerable to fakes and quick changes of direction.

4. Quickness

Players must make their moves quickly when faking. A ballcarrier can set up
a defender by appearing to relax a bit so the defender will also relax. Then a
quick fake step, followed by a quick "first" step will give the ballcarrier a half-
step on the defender, permitting the ballcarrier to drive to the net. If possible,
make this quick move before contact; the ballcarrier should try to keep space
between himself and his defender before starting his move.

REMEMBER: Stay low, make the step explosive and longer than
normal.

To make matters worse for the defender, the ballcarrier can choose the
moment to make his move, thereby providing an element of surprise in which
the defender, upon reacting to the ballcarrier's move, will have to make up for
a mental-reaction time lag, besides the physical-reaction time lag, because of
the suddenness of the move.

C. Fake Techniques

1. Outside Fake *(See Photos 20, 21)*

Ballcarrier fakes a cut to the outside, then cuts inside. This is called a strong-
side move and is the most common fake and most logical choice, as the ballcarrier quickly ends up in a good scoring position in the middle of the floor.

a.   The ballcarrier, on entering the Offensive Zone, must try to get his opponent moving backwards before giving him the "fake" move, i.e., stepping
outside and then cutting back in. He fakes as close to his check as possible without being cross-checked, so that his defender has less chance for
recovery. The key, though, is to get the defensive man moving backwards,
since he can't go in two directions — backwards and sideways — at the
same time.

b.   To execute the outside fake: when facing the defender at the beginning
of his move, the ballcarrier's stick will be exposed, but he keeps it vertical and in close to his body. On the fake step, he turns the stick inward
toward his body and turns his inside shoulder outward as if going to go
outside. On the "explosive" step, he turns his upper body in a 180-degree
turn back sideways. This puts the player in a good position to protect his
stick in case the defender reacts quickly enough to cross-check.

Another way of executing the outside fake is to keep the stick "still,"
held in a horizontal position, and rely more on the quickness of the fake
step to beat the defender.

c.   On giving the defensive man a small fake step, be sure to plant the right
foot outside of the defender's outside foot, then push off hard with this
right foot, and take a quick, large step with the left foot to the inside of the
floor. Stress stepping right and pushing left at a 90-degree angle (forming a
V-cut pattern). Dip the right shoulder to help "weasel" by the defender.

Variation: Instead of this V-cut, the ballcarrier does a Z-cut, where he plants
his inside foot first, then plants his outside foot. This is followed by a crossover
step with the outside foot to cut back into the middle. Reinforce that once the

Photo 20:
**The Outside
Fake —**
fake step outside

Photo 21:
**Outside
Fake —**
*explosive
step inside*

ballcarrier has planted his inside foot, he keeps it on the ground as he does a fake step and then a crossover step with his outside foot.

2. Inside Fake *(See Photos 22-24)*

Ballcarrier fakes a cut to the inside, then cuts outside.

a.   Recall this is a counter move for most players, but there are some players who are very successful using this "counter" move.

- The ballcarrier sets up the defender by giving him a small fake step to the inside, planting the left foot "outside" the defender's inside foot.

- Then the ballcarrier pushes off hard with the left foot and takes a quick, large step with the right foot to the outside.

Stress stepping left, then pushing right at a 90-degree angle (i.e., forming a V-cut pattern).

b. As the ballcarrier cuts outside, he turns his inside shoulder outwards and swings his stick across and to the outside of his body away from his defender to protect the stick. The ballcarrier accomplishes this by passing his stick to his right hand only — grabbing the stick about half-way up the shaft and resting the bottom half of the shaft on his forearm — and cradling the ball in the stick with the one hand, while still protecting the stick with his body. Some players prefer to swing the stick to the outside of their body, keeping both hands on the stick.

c. Once the ballcarrier gets his body beside his defender, he drops his inside shoulder and, using his inside arm, wards off his defender and "weasels" his way around in front of him, with the defender ending up on the ballcarrier's back.

d. The ballcarrier now switches the stick back to both hands, being aware that the defender is right behind him.

e. The ballcarrier has to use his body to protect his stick by holding it out in front of his body and shooting. If he brings the stick back over his shoulder to take his shot, he could be stick-checked by his defender. *(See Photo 25, p. 76.)*

Variation: Instead of the V-cut, the ballcarrier does a Z-cut, planting his outside foot, then planting his inside foot — the "fake" foot — as if he is going to cut back into the middle. This time, however, he keeps his outside foot (right foot) planted, and does a crossover step with his left foot and cuts to the outside.

3. Stutter Step to a Fake

The ballcarrier does a stutter step, which is many short steps in rapid succession, then jab steps (fake steps) with his right foot and accelerates to the left or vice versa. The ballcarrier tries to get the defender on the back of his heels, moving backwards, or leaning in one direction. The ballcarrier reacts to what the defense does; for example, if the defender commits in one direction, the ballcarrier goes in the opposite direction.

Photos 22-24:
The Inside Fake
Fake step inside ...

... step outside ...

... step beside the defender, swing stick outside, and "weasel" past him.

Photo 25:
Use the body
to protect the
stick.

D. The Fake-Shot or Stick-Fake *(See Photos 26, 27)*

- A ballcarrier uses the fake-shot to "freeze" or tighten up his defender giving himself a split-second advantage to go around.

- The fake-shot is used best when the defender tries to get his stick in the way of the ballcarrier's stick to interfere with his shot, or when a defender is rushing him.

- The fake-shot is accomplished as the ballcarrier goes to shoot his overhand shot. He turns his top-hand wrist inward to "check" his shot. Some players like to turn the stick outwards with their bottom-hand wrist on the fake (see chapter 9 — "Shooting"). The fake must look like the real thing, so the ballcarrier must pretend to actually shoot the ball, then at the last second "check" his shot.

  It is important to "sell the fake" to the opponent by making it look real; in other words, the fake looks like a fake or looks like the real thing. Looking at the net, and faking hard and quickly with the wrists. Stress that the player uses only his wrists.

  On a fake shot, the ballcarrier has the options of cutting across in front of the net, or cutting to the outside. More and more players are now using the fake shot, pulling the stick around in front of their body, cutting to the outside, and taking the shot.

- To execute the underhand fake shot, turn the top-hand wrist (which is now on the bottom of the shaft) upwards to "check" the shot.

Photo 26:
The Fake Shot
— *"check" shot and freeze defender.*

Photo 27:
The Fake Shot
— *cut across the top.*

E. Pivot

1. Inside Pivot

a. With the Defender Running Beside the Ballcarrier

In this strong-side move, balance and footwork are very important. A player uses his feet more in this move to beat his defender than in any other offensive move.

The left-shot ballcarrier fakes an outside drive with his outside foot, then plants his inside foot (left foot) in the middle of his defender's feet and spins back into the defender. The ballcarrier spins onto the defender's stick with his back and continues around, all the time pivoting on his inside foot. The outside foot is swung around, planted on the outside of the defender's inside foot, giving him good offensive positioning. When the ballcarrier is pivoting with his back to the defender, he must protect his stick by tucking it in close to his body and cradling it.

REMEMBER: Come out of the pivot in a good shooting position.

Variation: The ballcarrier fakes a drive to the outside and pivots quickly on his inside foot, spins around in front of his defender (preferably with no contact) and cuts across the top.

b. When Running Straight at a Set Defender

The left-shot ballcarrier plants his inside foot (left foot) between his defender's feet and fairly close to the defender's body. On the plant, turn the body sideways, turn the stick inward and tuck it in close to the body. Pivot on the planted foot, while at the same time pushing off with the outside foot (right foot). Then swing the right foot around the outside of the defender's inside foot. The ballcarrier should lean into his checker with his back as he executes this move.

REMEMBER: During the pivot, always keep the body between the
             checker and the stick.

The pivot is executed in a 180-degree turn. The ballcarrier goes as straight as possible when trying to beat his defender. If the ballcarrier goes in an arc on his pivot move, he will give his defender time and space to recover his defensive positioning (see photos on opposite page).

2. Outside Pivot

a. When Coming Out of the Corner (See Photos 31–33, p. 81)

In this counter move, the ballcarrier must make it appear he is working hard to go across the top to get a good shot off. He must run the defensive man hard toward the net, making sure he drives him high enough to give himself room for the outside pivot.

Plant the inside foot (right foot) in the middle of the defender's feet while swinging the outside foot (left foot) backwards, hooking on the outside of the defender's foot. Maintain contact with the back on the defender's stick during the pivot. At the end of the pivot, pass the stick to the outside hand (right hand), grabbing it in the middle of the shaft, while maintaining contact with

Photos 28-30:
Inside Pivot
Plant your inside foot between the defender's feet.

Pivot on planted foot, tuck stick in close and lean with your back.

Come out of pivot in shooting position.

the rest of the shaft on the forearm. The ballcarrier does this to protect the stick from the defender; at the same time, with this type of grip he can swing the stick out to cradle the ball in the stick.

As the ballcarrier finishes the 180-degree move, he hooks his inside elbow on the defender's back for leverage and dips his inside shoulder to "weasel" past his defender, eventually getting the defender on his back. Once he gets his defender on his back, the ballcarrier must bring his stick back around in front of his body to protect it.

b. When Running Straight at a Set Defender

The ballcarrier executes the outside pivot when the defender is overplaying the ballcarrier to stop him from cutting into the middle. The ballcarrier makes almost the same move as above, i.e., he plants his outside foot, pivots on it, and rolls back, swinging his inside foot around his defender.

F. Change of Pace

This move is used more when running the ball up the floor. The ballcarrier slows down or hesitates. Then, with a burst of speed, he explodes past his defender.

II. Tips for One-On-One Moves

1. One-on-one moves are attempted
    a. when running up the floor;
    b. when the play is still flowing into the Offensive Zone, and defensive players are not ready to help the teammate who is checking the ballcarrier;
    c. from a stationary position in the Offensive Zone; and
    d. when receiving a pass on a cut across the floor in the Offensive Zone.
2. An offensive player must take a "threat" position:
    a. Be balanced.
    b. Keep a good, wide stance only when taking a hit.
    c. Always keep the head up looking at the net and watching for any cutters going through the middle.
    d. Be in a position to go one-on-one or shoot the ball.
3. A great offensive player must be a scoring threat. he must be a player who can go one-on-one, shoot from the outside, pass as he is being cross-checked, and pass and cut quickly.

Photos 31-33:
Outside Pivot
*Plant outside
foot between
defender's feet.*

*Pivot, roll
back, swing-
ing inside
foot around
defender.*

*Pass stick to
outside hand.*

4. A player goes one-on-one to score or to beat his opponent to draw a teammate's defender, and then pass off to this open teammate.

5. The best time to go one-on-one is

    a. when the defender is not in a good defensive stance to check (i.e., his knees are not bent);

    b. when the defender is out of position;

    c. when the defender is tired;

    d. when the defender is overly aggressive and tries to get the ball from the ballcarrier by checking his stick and thus over-commits himself;

    e. when the defender rushes the ballcarrier, the ballcarrier can fake him or side-step him;

    f. when the defender reaches on his cross-check and over-commits;

    g. when the defender slashes and over-commits;

    h. when the ballcarrier's teammates are moving around occupying their men with the result of little or no backup;

    i. when the ballcarrier thinks he can beat his defender because of a mismatch (being bigger or quicker than the defender); or

    j. when the defender reacts to the ballcarrier's offensive move and makes a mistake or over-commits.

    Generally, in all of these situations, the ballcarrier "reads" the defender and reacts to his defensive mistake.

    > **Note** *Against a good defender, sometimes a ballcarrier can pass off and pick for a teammate, creating a switch, with the result of being picked up by a weaker check. Or he can have someone pick for him creating a switch, whereby he is picked up again by a weaker check.*

6. The best area to go one-on-one is from the ballcarrier's proper side of the floor in the Offensive Zone. If he beats his defender, especially with a strong-side move, he will be in the best shooting area — the middle of the floor. Whereas, if he goes one-on-one near the center of the floor and beats his defender, he will be in a poor shooting area and probably on his wrong side.

7. A good ballcarrier does not hang on to the ball too long. This strategy stops the offense and gives the defense time to back each other up. If

the ballcarrier cannot beat his check with his initial one-on-one move, he should pass off to create an off-ball play with his teammate on his side of the floor.

8. A good offensive player does not stand still, with or without the ball. If he keeps moving, he will be harder to hit and he will wear out his defender.

9. A great offensive player should have moves to go both ways. This becomes a big advantage as the defender cannot overplay his strong side.

10. A great offensive player learns to use his assets to the best of his ability to beat a defender. If he has size, he learns to use it; if he has speed, he learns to use it; if he has quickness, he learns to use it. Each player must find his own way to beat a defender (i.e., develop a favorite move, and develop a variety of counter moves in case the best move does not work or is taken away). Just don't become predictable.

11. The one-one-one confrontation is like a chess game in which the offensive player is always trying to set up his defender to beat him. The offensive man wants to keep the defensive man wondering what he is going to do. So, he pretends to do one thing and then does something else. The whole idea is to get the defender to react to the offensive player instead of the offensive player reacting to the defender.

12. Great one-on-one players have confidence in their ability to beat a defender; they are not intimidated by who the defender is or his size. This is often taken as cockiness, but most cocky players are exceptional one-on-one players.

13. It is important to remember that once a ballcarrier has beaten his check he must tuck in his stick in front of his body or he will be stick-checked from behind by his defender as a desperation move.

REMEMBER: Often enough, beating a man is done instinctively — don't think, just do it!

III. Individual Offensive Drills

A. Offensive Agility Drills (Footwork)

1. Faking

Players running in a straight line push with their right foot, then step ("explode") with their left foot. Continuing along, they then push with their left foot and step with their right foot. With this footwork they form V-cuts which are 90-degree change-of-direction moves.

2. Hopping

Players while hopping on their right foot only, push right and go left, then push left and go right. Players do the same movement with the left foot only, then on both feet.

3. Stutter Steps

Players running in a straight line do stutter steps which are steps in rapid succession, then push right, go left; stutter steps, then push left, go right.

4. Pivoting

Players running in a straight line, fake right, pivot, go left; then fake left, pivot, go right.

5. Agility Run

Players cut in and out between the cones placed 3–4 feet (1–2 metres) apart on the floor.

6. Skipping

Players go through a routine of skipping maneuvers.

7. Bench Jumping

Players jump sideways over benches with both feet together.

B. Drills to Teach Cradling the Ball

a. Stationary ballcarriers stand practicing cradling. Stress to players not to look at the ball, but to know where the ball is in their pocket by "feel" or weight.

b. Jogging ballcarriers run around the arena cradling a ball.

C. Drills to Teach Protecting the Stick

1. One-on-One Circle Drill

Checkers start the drill with their stick on the ballcarrier's body. On coach's command, the checkers try to stick-check the ballcarriers. The ballcarriers just pivot around in a circle cradling the ball and protecting their sticks.

Points to stress to the ballcarriers:

- look over their shoulders to watch the checkers rather than watching the ball in their sticks;
- hold the stick in a vertical position as opposed to a horizontal one, because it is easier to protect with the body;
- continuously cradle the stick.

Variation: The ballcarrier who protects his stick the longest (i.e., does not drop the ball) is the winner. All the other ballcarriers must do a token pushup for losing.

2. One-on-Two Circle Drill

This is the same as the One-on-One Circle Drill, but two checkers go after the ballcarrier's stick. The key here is to neutralize one of the checkers by leaning on his stick. Then the ballcarrier just concentrates on the other checker.

3. Tag Game

The chaser is "it" and has no ball. Everybody else in the group (5–10 players) has a ball. Play the game in a restricted area. "It" chases the ballcarriers to try to force them out of bounds or to drop the ball. If a ballcarrier steps out of bounds or drops his ball, then that player is "it."

4. British Bulldog Game

Coach makes up two teams: one team is at center; the other has balls at one end of the floor. On a call of "Bulldog," the ballcarriers run from one end of the floor to the other. The defensive players try to check as many ballcarriers as possible by dislodging the ball. The defensive team that forces the most dropped balls wins.

Variation: When a ballcarrier loses his ball he becomes part of the defensive team; the last player with a ball is the winner.

D. Drills to Teach Taking a Hit

1. Bump Drill

Players are paired up as a ballcarrier and a defensive player. The defensive player has no stick. The defender tries to jar the ball loose by pushing sharply with both hands on the ballcarrier's body.

This drill teaches ballcarriers to

- relax with the ball when taking a cross-check;
- take a wide stance when receiving a cross-check; and
- lean into the direction the force (cross-check) comes from.

*Variation:*The defender uses his body (upper shoulder) to bang against the ballcarrier's body, trying to jar the ball loose.

2. Equalizing Pressure Drill

a.   Players are still in partners.The ballcarrier cuts across the top while absorbing a straight push by the defender's hands on his upper arm.

b.   The defender then cross-checks as the ballcarrier cuts across the top, gradually increasing the intensity of the cross-checks so the ballcarrier gets the feel of a hard check. Players should relax their body, lean into the check, and look at the net.

3. Charging Defender Drill

This drill teaches how to avoid taking a hit. Ballcarriers have to learn not to panic when a defender charges them, but to see this as a defensive mistake and use it to their advantage. All an offensive player does is side-step the defender, fake one way, and go the other way. In this drill the defenders charge the ballcarrier, with the ballcarrier practicing a side-step.

4. Gauntlet Drill

The ballcarrier zig-zags around the defensive players spaced out in a straight line.The ballcarrier works on

a.   balance (wide stance);

b.   quickness (footwork)

c.   turning sideways to use the body to protect the stick;

d.   keeping his head up to see the floor and his defender (rather than watching the ball in the stick); and

e.   relaxing when taking a hit (rather than tensing up).

In this gauntlet drill the offense always wins, in order to give them the confidence in their offensive skills. The defenders take it easy at the beginning, even to the point where they just fake the move.

On the coach's command the defender will stick-check when the ball carrier is in front of him (one attempt); cross-check only (one attempt); or cross-check lightly, let the ballcarrier go by him, then try to stick check from behind.The ballcarrier reacts to each situation accordingly.

E. Drills to Teach Offensive Moves

The ballcarrier practices his offensive moves against his partner:

• Inside Slide Move (Taking a Hit)

- Outside Slide Move (Inside Spin Move option)
- Roll Move
- Outside Fake Move
- Inside Fake Move
- Stutter Step to a Fake Move
- Fake Shot and Go
- Inside Pivot
- Bull Move
- Bait Move
- Outside Pivot
- Change of Pace

Progression:

i) Neither player has a stick as the offensive player practices his moves.

ii) Only the offensive player has his stick.

iii) Both players have their sticks, but the offensive player works against token defense.

F. Shooting Off an Offensive Move Drill

Coach forms two lines (left shots, right shots) with a cone in front of each line. The cone is placed just inside the Prime Scoring Area Side Boundary Line *(see Diagram 12, p. 90)* at about 15 feet (4.5 m) from the crease or closer, depending on the age group. Everybody has a ball. The players in each line attack the cones straight on, without touching the cones, using the offensive moves the coach asks for.

As players work on offensive moves, stress deception, quickness, good footwork, and taking the shot a player would take in a game.

Offensive moves to use in this drill:

- Outside Fake
- Inside Fake
- Stutter Step to a Fake
- Fake Shot and Go
- Inside Pivot
- Outside Pivot
- Change of Pace

G. One-on-One Offensive Moves against Common Defensive Mistakes

In this drill, the defense purposely makes common mistakes so that the offense can learn how to deal with them. This will give the offensive player confidence when he meets these situations in a game.

a. Defender slashes at ballcarrier — when the defender over-commits, the ballcarrier makes his move.

b   Defender tries to check ballcarrier's stick — when the defender over-commits, the ballcarrier side-steps him, protects his stick, and goes to the net.

c. Defender is moving backwards — ballcarrier fakes one way and cuts in the opposite direction.

d. Defender reaches on cross-check — ballcarrier side-steps him and goes to the net.

e. Defender rushes or charges the ballcarrier — ballcarrier fakes one way and goes the other way.

f. Defender players the ballcarrier straight on — ballcarrier now has two ways to go.

g. Defender overplays the ballcarrier from cutting across the top — ballcarrier fakes inside, then cuts outside, or fakes an outside cut, then cuts back inside.

h. Defender leans or pushes on ballcarrier with his stick to stop him from going to the net, or to force him in a certain direction — ballcarrier's options:

   • He rolls back and forth with his back and shoulders on the defender's stick to get a reaction; once the defender commits in a direction to cut off the roll, the ballcarrier goes past him in the opposite direction (see section on the Roll Move, p. 69)

   • He beats the defender physically by sliding past him off his stick while working on getting his shoulder and body on the inside of the checker's stick (see section on the Slide Move, p. 67).

   • He steps back to get defender off-balance, then steps by him.

i. Defender is standing still (planted) — ballcarrier beats him on a quickness move.

j. Defender is playing ballcarrier tight — ballcarrier beats him on a quickness move.

k. Defender is playing ballcarrier very loose — ballcarrier's options:

- He can fake a long shot and go to the net.
- With the space already created, he can just shoot.
- He can get closer to the defender, or go to an area where he will be played tighter, then beat the defender on quickness.

H. One-on-One Competitive Drills

1. One-on-One from Side of Floor

Form four lines on the floor: two defensive lines and two offensive lines. The one defensive line and the one offensive line are all right-shots on the left side of the floor; the other defensive line and offensive line are all left shots on the right side of the floor. The first left-shot defender throws a diagonal pass to the right-shot offensive player, touches his body with his stick, then the ballcarrier makes his offensive move. This drill also reinforces that a defender has to pick up an opposite shot to himself, so that his stick can interfere with the ballcarrier's stick.

Variations:

a. Defender can use no stick at first; then he can use a stick later to play defense. He throws a diagonal pass with his hand.

b. As soon as the offensive player receives the ball, he goes for the net and does not wait for the defender to touch him.

c. Ballcarrier beats the defender facing him only. He cannot turn his back to the defender.

d. Ballcarrier beats the defender only after receiving a cross-check.

e. Ballcarrier beats the defender while the defender is "closing out" (see chapter 8 on Individual Defense).

f. Ballcarrier must beat defender in five seconds.

2. One-on-One from Center of Floor

Stress in this drill that the ballcarrier should move to his proper side of the floor before he makes his offensive move.

Variations:

a. Coach can run the drill in the Offensive Zone or the full-length of the floor.

b. Ballcarrier beats defender from Defensive Zone of the floor. To start the

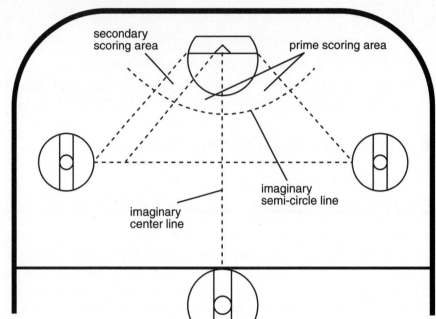

secondary
scoring area

prime scoring area

imaginary
semi-circle line

imaginary
center line

Diagram 12

Prime scoring area for a left-shot player.

drill, the defender passes to the offensive man. Then he is pressured all the way down the floor.

c. Offensive player must get in the clear from the defensive pressure for the pass from the goalie. Then he is pressured all the way down the floor.

3. "Showdown" Game

Two teams are chosen (rights vs. lefts, or picked teams) for a one-on-one competition. Coach to stress offense — just reinforces offensive players.

If offense scores, team gets 3 points. If offense beats the defender and gets a good shot on net, but does not score, team gets 2 points. If offense cannot beat the defender or get a good shot on net, team gets 0 points. Teams play to 15 points. Losers do pushups.

— 8 —
Individual Defense (Cross-Checking)

I. Why Cross-Check?

• To prevent the ballcarrier from going to the net.

• To stop the ballcarrier from getting a good shot on net, or, at least, to interfere with his shot.

• To force the ballcarrier into errors through pressure (e.g., forcing a bad pass, or "coughing up" the ball).

• To force the ballcarrier to go where the defender wants him to go, usually towards the boards.

• To force the ballcarrier to turn his back to the play.

• To worry the ballcarrier so that he becomes more concerned with protecting the ball than beating his man.

• To harass the ballcarrier so he does not have time to see the plays developing on the floor.

II. Cross-Check Technique

A. Floor Positioning
B. Cross-Check Stance
C. Holding the Stick
D. Footwork

E. Before Contact

F. Actual Contact

A. Floor Positioning

Positioning Rule: "Head on the Stick" This means the defender plays between his opponent's stick and the net forming an imaginary straight line with the stick, the defender, and the net.

To get to this position, the defender angles out on the ballcarrier with his shoulders at a 45-degree angle to the boards, picking up the offensive player on his inside shoulder to encourage him to the side boards. In this overplay position, the defender wants

- to stop the ballcarrier from cutting across the top of the floor (i.e., to take away his strong-side move);
- to give the ballcarrier only one way to go;
- to force the ballcarrier into his counter or secondary move; and
- to force the ballcarrier to the boards.

B. Cross-Check Stance

Take a position of "readiness" — be ready to move laterally or backwards. This

Photo 34:
The Defensive Stance

physical position is also called the "athletic stance" or the "fighter's stance."

1. The feet are staggered both facing in the same direction. Keep your feet a little wider than shoulder-width apart for a good solid base.

2. Keep your weight on the balls of your feet (be bouncy) so you won't get caught flat-footed.

3. Keep your head up for balance. Keep your eyes focused on the top of the chest area or on the top of the numbers, as this helps to keep your head up.

4. Stay low, keeping the rear down, the back slightly bent and the knees bent. This position gives a player a lower center of gravity, providing better balance and a stronger base, enabling him to move in any direction quicker.

Players should never bend at the waist, since this causes them to become off-balance more easily; and they should never stand up straight, as this gives them a higher center of gravity, making it harder to move quickly.

C. Holding the Stick

In the cross-checking grip the hands are placed farther apart than one normally would hold the stick when passing. Cock the arms in anticipation of cross-checking. The "open face" of the stick should be facing backwards, so that the stick is in a better position, by turning the stick slightly, to pick up any loose balls. It is also important to turn the stick a quarter of a turn so the play-

Photo 35:
The Retreat Step — *ballcarrier tries to beat the defender outside.*

er is checking against the grain of the aluminum or titanium and will not end up bending the shaft from hitting.

D. Footwork

1. Retreat Step vs. Cut to Outside *(See Photo 35)*

By forcing the ballcarrier one way (outside), the checker can anticipate in which direction he is going. The defender takes this staggered stance with the inside foot forward and the outside foot back. This staggered stance allows the defender to push off with his front foot and step with his back foot to go backwards (retreat step) which is usually the direction the ballcarrier is going.

Stress turning the knee of the inside foot inward and putting weight on the inside of the inside foot to push off with; and maintain part of the foot on the ground, rather than picking it up, for speed and quickness.

2. Drop Step to a Shuffle Step vs. Cut to Inside *(See Photo 36)*

If a ballcarrier fakes outside, then cuts across the top, the defender must have a counter move to change direction. A player uses a "drop step" technique in which he steps backwards with the inside foot and then moves both feet laterally to cut the ballcarrier off from going to the net. He shuffles with quick, short, lateral side steps, yet keeps his feet spread to provide a solid base. If the feet come together, he will lose balance and strength; and if the feet cross, he may trip himself.

Photo 36:
The Drop Step to a Shuffle — *ballcarrier tries to cut across the top.*

3. Attack Step

The attack step is used when filling a gap between the defender and ballcarrier or when "closing out." Closing out is when the defender rushes out at his check or when he receives a pass. He arrives at an angle, to force to the boards, and shuffles the last two steps.

E. Before Contact

Points to stress to defenders before contact:

- Wait for the ballcarrier to come to you. Reaching or lunging for the ballcarrier may cause you to lose your balance

- Stay in a crouched position, possibly even getting lower than the ballcarrier. Never stand fully upright when cross-checking. The defender will have a harder time moving laterally with his legs straight, plus he could be knocked off-balance with this higher center of gravity.

- Watch the ballcarrier's chest rather than the ball. If the defender watches the ball, he will usually end up stick checking, thereby over-committing.

- When getting ready to hit, do not tense your muscles completely. Tensing up will slow down your cross-checking movement.

F. Actual Contact *(See Photo 37)*

Points to stress to defenders on contact:

- Keep the head up and over the groin area. This helps a defender stay balanced.

- Be stationary on the hit. This gives the checker a solid base for a powerful hit; as well, he will be ready to move laterally if he needs to. If he is moving backwards, and the ballcarrier cuts across the top, it is harder to recover (i.e., to move sideways). The defender cannot move in two directions at the same time (i.e., backwards and sideways).

- Take a slight step with the forward foot.

- From the crouched position, extend the arms upwards and outwards on the hit. Many times, if a player cross-checks straight out with the arms, it means he is standing up. Stay low on the hit.

- Make the hit short and hard, then recoil the stick. Cross-check and recover (i.e., get the stick back ready to hit again). On the cross-check, try to keep the ballcarrier in the middle of the stick, between both hands.

  Note *If the ballcarrier is allowed to lean on the defender's stick, it is easier for him to roll, to make the defense overreact, or to shoot around the defender.*

- Fill the gap created by the hit between the two players, take little steps forward, stay down and continue hitting.

- Lean forward slightly more when cross-checking a rushing ballcarrier to absorb the force of the contact.

- After contact with the cross-check, when the player has to maintain contact with the ballcarrier so he doesn't get beat, he might have to use the upper part of his arms and shoulders, bent out to the side, to give himself more leverage and body width in helping to stop the ballcarrier.

III. Individual Defensive Strategies

1. Picking Up a Check

Usually a left-handed shot picks up a right-handed shot to check and vice versa. This is so the defender ends up in a stick-on-stick position which makes it easier to interfere with the opponents shot or pass.

When checking a ballcarrier out of the scoring area, bother him by slapping at his stick to interfere with the accuracy of his pass, but remain down in the defensive stance in case he decides to go one-on-one. If the ballcarrier is running towards the defender, but out of the scoring area, the defender must start moving as the ballcarrier approaches to pick up momentum to match the ballcarrier's speed, but when it is time to cross-check, the checker must make sure he is stationary.

Photo 37:
The Cross-Check

2. Closing Out

Closing out occurs when a defender has to rush his check, usually on receiving a cross-floor pass, to maintain pressure and to stop the ballcarrier from scoring. He accomplishes this by getting his body directly in front of the ballcarrier's stick and trying to arrive at the same time as the ball does, under control and balanced.

3. If Defender is Beaten

If the ballcarrier beats the defender one-on-one, the defender shouldn't panic. Instead, he should wait for the ballcarrier's stick to come back in preparation to shoot; then all he has to do is knock the ballcarrier's stick down or up.

4. Defensive Reminders

- Make sure all shots taken are molested (i.e., interferred with, pressured, hurried).

- Don't slash the ballcarrier because of the chance of a penalty being called and the danger of over-committing.

- Don't stick check (trying to steal the ball from the ballcarrier). The defender gets beaten too easily, too many times, because of this over-commitment.

- Don't get impatient and go after the ballcarrier. By cross-checking too early the defender reaches and becomes off-balance.

- When cross-checking and the ballcarrier passes off, never "finish your check" or gives him one more cross-check. The defender now puts himself out of the play. Once his check passes the ball, the defender should try to help on the ball and still be aware of where his check is.

IV. Tips for Being a Great Defensive Player

- The main thing in playing defense is "wanting" to play it. To play good defense a player must have a certain attitude; he must be a relentless worker; he must love to hit; he must be aggressive.

- A great defensive player realizes having good floor position saves a lot of unnecessary work.

- A great defensive player must
  a. have the proper technique for stopping a ballcarrier (technique is more important than strength);
  b. be physically ready;

    c. be mentally ready and alert;

    d. have outstanding lateral and backward mobility;

    e. have good body balance.

- A great defensive player must have good concentration. He must be totally involved in the game, especially when his opponent doesn't have the ball.

- A great defensive player must try to out-think his offensive man by anticipating his moves; by knowing his opponent, and what to expect of him. He should know his opponent's strength and favorite moves:

    a. Does he think "score" or "pass"?

    b. Does he like to take long shots or shoot close in?

    c. How good an outside shooter is he?

    d. How well does he go to his left? His right?

    e. Does he move quickly laterally?

    f. Does he handle the ball with poise and confidence, or does he get rattled under pressure?

V. Individual Defensive Drills: Defending Against the Man with the Ball

Some tips on defensive drills:

- Defense is something a coach can teach players, whereas offensive moves are sometimes just the result of a player's natural talent. Any player can be a great defensive player if he wants to be.

- To teach defense, the coach should control what the offense does in the drill.

- In the beginning of defensive drills, defense should always win. As the defensive player's skills improve, create drills that give defenders a tougher time than in actual game situations.

1. Defensive Agility Drills (Quick Feet Drills)

a. Running Backwards

b. Carioca
While moving sideways to the right, step over the right foot with the left foot and then step behind the right foot with the left foot while maintaining the

upper body facing in the same direction all the time. Then repeat still facing in the same direction, stepping with the right foot.

c. Step Over
While running forward in a straight line, step in front of each foot.

d. Front Crossover
While moving sideways, one foot steps behind the other foot continuously.

e. Back Crossover
While moving sideways, one foot steps behind the other foot continuously.

f. Quarter Jump Turns (90-degree turns, 180-degree turns)

2. Defensive Stance Drill
Players stay in defensive stance position for a designated time (60 seconds).

3. Defensive Slide Drill
Players slide between two cones 10 feet (3 m) apart while the coach counts the number of slides in 30 seconds.

4. Wave Drill (Footwork)
Players react to hand motion of coach (front, backwards, sideways).

5. Shadow Drills (Footwork)
a.   Partners mirror each other.
b.   Defensive partners react to offensive partners:
   i)   Ballcarrier cuts to outside; defender pushes off with front foot to cut off ballcarrier (retreat step).
   ii) Ballcarrier cuts to inside, defender with first step, cuts off the ballcarrier by taking a Drop Step and then Shuffle-steps sideways, keeping the ballcarrier from going to the net. This is a drill of first steps: the defender works on quickness and body balance.

6. "Checking the Ballcarrier without a Stick" Drill
Checkers (without their sticks) hold on to the front of their sweaters. Using only their forearms, upper arms, and body, they make contact with the ballcarriers to stop them from scoring. Checkers cannot grab the ballcarriers with their hands. Stress staying low, balanced, and shuffling sideways quickly.

a.   From the middle of the floor and side of the floor, the defensive player forces the ballcarrier to his weak side and to the boards.

b.   From deep in the corner area, the defensive player forces the ballcarrier to the middle of the floor where he should get help from his teammates in a game. A player does not force the ballcarrier to the boards when the ballcarrier is in the corner, because if he is beaten to the outside he will have no help.

7. "Battle" Drill

This is one-on-one checking using sticks. Players use old sticks so they don't have to worry about breaking their game sticks.

Players battle to beat or stop their opponents. Drill has four lines: two offensive lines and two defensive lines; left shots stay on one side of the floor and rotate from offense to defense and vice versa for the right shots. All the defenders have a ball.

To start the drill, the defender throws a diagonal pass to the opposite side of the floor. Defender then goes and touches the ballcarrier's body with the end of this stick and the drill begins *(see p. 89)*.

8. "Showdown" Game

This is a competition between two teams, usually lefties versus righties. Coach stresses defense and reinforces the defensive players. Players get a point from stopping the offense from scoring. The first team to 10 points wins.

9. "Steal the Ball" Drill

Sometimes during a game a team needs to gamble to get the ball. In this drill the defender practices getting the ball off the ballcarrier. The defender has to play "cat-and-mouse" with the ballcarrier faking to get the ball, and being deceptive.

— 9 —
Shooting

Although there are three main shooting techniques — overhand shooting (similar to an axe-swinging motion), side arm shooting (similar to swinging a baseball bat; see p. 124), and underhand shooting (similar to a golf swing) — the overhand shot will be dealt with here because the overhand shot complements the overhand pass, which works well with the Fast-Break System.

I. Overhand Long-Ball Shooting Technique

Note *What makes this shooting technique so simple is that a player imitates the same motion used in overhand passing.*

Overhand Long-Ball Shooting Check List

A. Stance

B. Grip of Stick

C. Shooting Position of Stick

D. Cocking of the Stick, or "Winding Up"

E. Release of Ball

F. Follow-through

A. Stance

1. The side of the shooter's body faces the net at a 45-degree angle.
2. Keeping the knees bent and taking a wide stance will give a shooter good body balance, thereby affording a better stance to get power into his shot.
3. The feet should be ready to shoot. The front foot (foot on opposite side of stick) is at a 45-degree angle to the net and the back foot is parallel to the net with most of the body weight on it.

B. Grip of Stick

1. Hold the stick with the fingers, but loosely to get the "feel" (soft hands).
2. The top-hand arm is the "power and guide" arm in the shot and the bottom-hand arm is the "stabilizer." Both arms are flexed at the beginning of the shot.
3. Positions of the hands do not have to change for passing or shooting. (Remember: The top hand is just below the mid-point of the shaft.) Some overhand shooters slide their top hand down to get the hands closer together, approximately 5 inches (2.5 cm), for a better "whip" motion in their shot. By bringing the hands closer together, a player gets more momentum into his shot because he can drop his stick back farther behind his body. The farther the head of the stick has to rotate, the more "whip" he gets into his shot. He may, however, lose some control over his stick if he brings his hands too close together on the overhand shot.

   Note   *Do not hold your stick tight at the start of your shot.*

C. Shooting Position of Stick

The stick can be held in one of three positions: straight up and down, straight back at a 45-degree angle to the floor, or parallel to the floor.

The height the stick is held varies with individuals. Overhand shooting players like to hold the stick high, with the top hand level with their head. Other players like to hold the stick a little lower, with the top hand parallel to the chin.

But whatever the preference, a player should hold his stick at the same level for all overhand shots. Some players have a tendency to hold the stick high for high shots and low for low shots, which allows the goalie to predict the shot.

D. Cocking of the Stick, or "Winding Up" *(See Photo 38)*

1. The shooter cocks the stick by flexing both of the wrists backwards and moving the stick farther back with both arms. The top-hand arm should be fully extended. This position will help get more momentum into the shot. At the same time, the shooter steps 4 inches (10 cm) with his front foot to give himself a good, wide, solid base for power.

2. The stick is now held horizontally or at a slight 45-degree angle to the floor and over the stick shoulder. the butt of the stick is now pointing at the target.

    Note *When an overhand shooter has a deeper pocket, he has to drop his stick back farther behind his body to get more whip (power) and a higher trajectory into his shot.*

3. Good players adjust their stick's netting so the ball goes to the same spot — the shooting pocket — every time. Players might do a small cradle just before shooting to check, by the weight of the ball, that it is still in the shooting pocket.

    Although players try to catch and shoot from the same spot in the pocket, they sometimes catch the ball in the middle or at the throat end of the pocket by mistake. This forces them to do a small cradle or drop the head of the stick below the butt end to roll the ball into the shooting pocket, just before they shoot.

Photo 38: Winding up for the overhand shot

REMEMBER: The shooting pocket is usually at the tip of the stick on the edge of the last shooting string.

E. Release of Ball *(See Photo 39)*

1. It is important to begin the shot with the body weight on the planted back foot; as the player takes another small step (6 inches/15 cm) with his front foot the body weight is transferred to this foot. This transfer of weight and wider stance helps to put more power into the shot.

2. Shooters like to take a slight hop with the rear foot, and then step with the front foot. This slight hopping motion with the rear foot helps to put rhythm into the shot and gets everything into sync.

3. The shooter pulls the stick from behind his shoulder by extending his top-hand arm forward and snapping both wrists forward. (Remember: He should keep his bottom-hand arm flexed, even though he snaps the wrist forward.) The quicker and stronger the swinging motion of the stick, the more momentum it will pick up, making for a more powerful shot. Stress being a "wrist" shooter rather than a "pusher." A pusher is a player who has a tendency to hold the stick too high on the shaft with the top hand and extends both arms to release the ball. Stress sliding the top hand down when shooting.

4. Early release of the ball when it is still behind the body produces a high and level trajectory. This release is exaggerated more when a shooter

Photo 39: Release of the ball for the overhand shot

wishes to compensate for a "hook." Late release of the ball produces a low trajectory (i.e., the ball will be released when it is beside or in front of the body). This is a very common mistake for beginning players.

F. The Ideal Follow-through *(See Photo 40)*

1. Ideally, the shooter should end up with a full extension of his top-hand arm, and with the butt of his stick touching his top-hand arm elbow, but in reality, a player will end up at a slight angle rather than straight ahead.

2. The head of the stick ends up pointing at the target as if the shooter were following the ball into the net with his stick.

3. Body weight ends up on the front foot.

4. To get the full weight of his body behind the shot, the shooter should make sure his shoulders and hips end up facing square to the net.

II. Tips for Successful Shooting

A. Knowing What a Good Shot Is

Good shot selection helps to obtain a high shooting percentage, which is one of the most important statistics in lacrosse.

*Photo 40:
Follow-through
for the
overhand shot*

1. Location on the Floor

As the angle of the shot is important, the shooter should know the best position on the floor to score from, called the "Prime Scoring Area." It is a good idea to measure and mark the high percentage spots on the floor with an X. *(See Diagram 12 on p. 90.)*

2. Distance

Shooters should shoot in their range, but they should find their range in practice, not during a game. They should shoot relaxed. If they do not shoot in their range, they will just "bomb" or force their shots. For most long-ball shooters, the area around the imaginary semi-circle line (15 ft./4.5 m) is a good shot. After beating a defender, a ballcarrier tends to want to beat one more defender to get in closer to the net for a better shot and end up getting double-teamed by the defense. Players must understand that they do not have to be right at the crease for a good shot.

3. Defensive Pressure

A shooter that is "open" will get a better shot off than if closely checked. The shooting rule is a shooter's stick cannot be interferred with on the shot, no stick or body in front of the shot. Shooters do not shoot around opponents, called screened shots, unless the defenders are playing off of them and they cannot interfere with their stick.

4. Discipline Shooting

The shooter must have patience when shooting and use good judgment in taking shots. He does not rush his shot, but takes a split second to look where he is going to shoot. Shooting discipline means that if a shooter doesn't have a good shot, he doesn't shoot; if he doesn't see an "opening" to shoot at, he doesn't shoot. A lot of players end up just shooting at the goalie.

5. Knowing the Goalie

The shooter should know how the goalie reacts to stick-fakes, and how he plays different shots. He should also know the type of goalie he is shooting against — an angle goalie or a reflex goalie (give a spot and take it away).

> **Note**   *In the game of lacrosse, the ball is played in the air, so shots are not usually deflected or screened. Therefore, it is extremely important to stress high-percentage shooting.*

B. Being Ready to Shoot for a Quicker Release

1. Being physically and mentally prepared to shoot the ball before receiving it is very important.

   Note *Before catching the ball, the experienced long-ball shooter puts his stick's target back behind his body with both arms extended backwards in a "cocked" position ready to shoot. Only experienced players should think about their shots before catching the ball. Beginners should concentrate on catching the ball first, then shooting.*

2. Getting into a good scoring position before receiving the ball saves time.

3. Having the stick up and ready to catch and shoot, not down at the side, is necessary while on offense.

4. Having the feet ready to shoot is key. The lead foot is out in front before the ball is caught.

5. After catching the ball, the player has two choices depending on the situation:

   a. He can shoot without cocking the stick or taking a step when cutting across the top or when he does not have much time to shoot.

   b. He can take the stick back to cock it, turn the body to face the net, and step with the front foot into the shot when he is completely open and has time to shoot.

C. Shooting Progression

Follow these steps to hone shooting skills:

1. Develop good form first.

2. Develop accuracy next. Placement of the shot is more important than power in a shot. If the shot is released and correctly placed, no goalie will stop it. Work on consistency through repetition.

3. Work on speed or power third. Too much emphasis is put on power when a combination of power and accuracy is needed.

4. Work on seeing the whole net, yet concentrating on the target.

5. Finally, work on deception and faking.

1. Using Good Shooting Technique

Player does not worry about putting the ball in the net at this stage. *(See section on Overhand Long-Ball Shooting Technique, p. 101–105.)*

2. Accuracy

a. Work on accuracy over speed (power). This is the most important part of shooting. The shooter has to learn to "pick" or place his shot for the open spot rather than just shooting at the net ("bombing" his shot). Players must understand that long shots do not have to be hard to go in; accuracy and deception are far more important.

b. The shooter has to learn to pause a second after he gets the ball so he does not rush his shot. This slight hesitation will give him time to take a quick look to pick his spot and then shoot.

c. Occasionally a shooter may not have time to look at his target, or he knows by intuition that he has an opening. As soon as the ball hits his pocket, he should shoot. This quick release before the goalie is set is called a "quick stick" and is a very underrated shot. The quick stick can be used effectively on long shots, particularly against a goalie who does not move well laterally.

3. Power

a. Once a shooter gets accuracy, he must then work on the hardness or speed of his shot. He must learn to "explode" into his shot.

b. The shooter gets power into his shot by

   i) The position of the ball in the pocket. Shooting the ball at the tip of his stick, on the last shooting string, rather than in the middle of the pocket, will give more power into his shot.

   ii) Using his legs — taking a wide stance and moving his body weight from his back foot to his front foot to get his body weight behind his shot. This weight transfer is one of the most effective ways of generating stick speed, which gives the shot power.

   iii) "Cocking" or moving the stick farther back. This gets more momentum into his shot. The top-hand arm takes the stick straight back.

   iv) Moving the hands slightly closer together, putting more momentum into the shot.

   v) Pulling the stick straight forward with the top-hand arm and snapping the cocked wrists forward gives more whip, generating more power in the shot. Here, the bottom hand holds the stick tighter and thereby becomes more involved in the shot.

vi) Rotating the hips and shoulders quickly.

vii) Having a good follow-through by fully extending the top-hand arm, resulting in the tip of the stick facing the target.

viii) Stepping through with the back foot on the follow-through.

c. The great shooters can shoot the ball faster than a goalie can move, therefore it should be stressed to players to just shoot for the open spots.

> **Note** *The problem with beginning players is that many have a tendency to shoot at the goalie rather than at the open spots. Stress to beginners to try to miss the goalie rather than aiming for a spot.*

4. Concentrate on the Target

On a straight shot, shooters must learn to concentrate on the target, yet not "telegraph" their shot. They must see the whole net using their peripheral vision, yet not look directly at where they're going to shoot , because some goalies watch a shooter's eyes.

> **Note** *The shooter's near side or the goalie's short side is the side of the net closest to the ball. The shooter's far side or the goalie's long side is the side of the net farthest from the ball (see Diagram 13, next page).*

5. Deception (Faking)

When stick-faking, the shooter should try to dictate the shot rather than letting the goalie determine it, because some goalies like to give the shooter a spot to shoot at, then take it away.

So, when shooting, the player should have a pre-conceived idea before he shoots to try to move the goalie, get a reaction from him, or at least "freeze" him (i.e., the goalie will tighten up because he thinks a shot is coming). Usually the stick-fake is the bad angle (setting the goalie up) and the shot is the good angle.

The key in stick-faking is to be deceptive: faking with the body, the stick, and the eyes. He should do something out of the ordinary that a goalie would seldom think of.

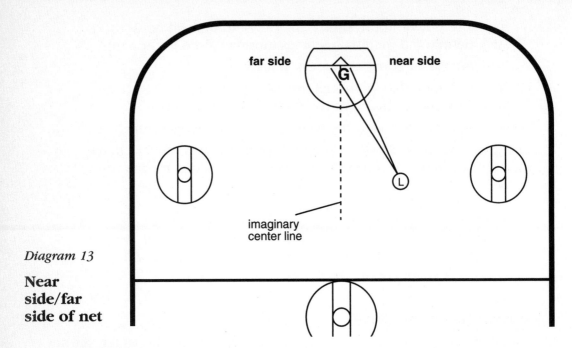

Diagram 13

Near side/far side of net

a. Long-Ball Overhand Fake Shot

i) The Stick-Fake

From a hard overhand, stick-fake back into an overhand shot, or from a hard overhand, stick-fake into a fluid sidearm shot. A player "fakes" his overhand shot by starting the forward motion of his stick as if he is really going to shoot, then he "checks" his shot by rotating inward strongly with his top-hand wrist and lightly with his bottom-hand wrist. Basically, the top hand grips the stick fairly tight for control and the bottom hand holds the stick loosely so that the stick can rotate easily in the grip. This turning motion of the wrist with the top hand turns the stick clockwise, keeping the ball in the netting. It is important this motion is done quickly and hard to make it look real. The shooter must "sell the product." Speed and fluidity are very important in stick-faking.

Variation 1: Some players like to stick-fake using their bottom hand as the power hand. The bottom-hand wrist turns inward, rotating the stick counter-clockwise. The stick just turns in the top-hand grip.

Variation 2: To counter a goalie watching his eyes, a shooter can look at the far corner and pretend to shoot at that corner by holding the "face" of the stick at the far corner. This is not a fake-shot motion — more of a hesitation. As he brings the stick off his shoulder, he turns the stick inwards and in one continuous motion continues with his stick to the near corner.

ii) Body Fake

To complement the stick-fake, the shooter can make the goalie think he is going to shoot at the goalie's short side by dropping his front shoulder making it look like he is going to shoot at this near corner, but instead of pulling his stick across his body, he continues to swing the stick straight ahead and shoots at the far side of the net.

iii) Eye Fake

When stick-faking, the ballcarrier should always look at the corner at which he is faking, since some goalies watch the shooter's eyes to anticipate the shot. For example, to counter a goalie watching his eyes, a shooter can look at the far corner and fake a shot at that corner, then shoots at the near corner.

b. Long-Ball Sidearm Fake-Shot

From a hard sidearm stick-fake into a fluid, quick overhand shot, or from a hard sidearm stick-fake into a sidearm shot. This sidearm stick-fake is the same wrist motion as the overhand stick-fake. The shooter must make sure on the "checking" of the shot that he turns his top-hand wrist up strongly.

> **Note** *It is hard to make a complete fake shot when shooting the underhand shot. But a player through his body language can fake a shot by dipping his front shoulder and shaking his stick as if he is going to shoot.*

D. Shooting Strategy

1. Great shooters like to catch and shoot from the same spot in the pocket.

2. On the release of the ball from the pocket, some shooters want the ball to run out smoothly in the pocket; some like to feel the ball "tick" the top of the plastic mouth to know it has gone; and others like it to touch the shooting strings.

3. A player can use a variety of shots in a game (overhand, underhand, sidearm), but usually he uses the shot he feels most comfortable with through practice.

4. Mixing up the shot placement is very important when shooting. The shooter wants to keep the goalie wondering where he is going to place his shot: at the corners, off the hips, under the glove hand, between the legs, or off the ankles.

    The shooter can make it a straight shot or a bounce shot. Bounce shots are very underrated and very difficult for a goalie to stop. If a shooter sees no open top spots, he should bounce the ball down by the side of the goalie's foot.

5. It is also important to know the goalie's weaknesses, his favorite moves,

and whether he is an angle goalie or a reflex goalie (one that likes to bait a ballcarrier into shooting at an open spot, then take it away).

If he is an angle goalie, the shooter can fake but he won't get a reaction, so he better be ready to pick a spot and shoot, whereas a reflex goalie will go for the fake. Most reflex goalies will give the shooter the short side of the net because it is usually the shorter distance to move to cover. A shooter should have a counter to this "give and take away" move by the goalie. For example, if a goalie gives a left-handed shooter his left side of the net (short side) to shoot at, the shooter, while winding up, will look at the short side, slightly drop his right shoulder, and hesitate a split-second with his stick. These moves will give the goalie the impression that the shooter is going to come across his body with his stick and throw the ball into the short side. As the goalie starts to move across to cover the short side of the net, instead of pulling the stick across his body, the shooter will continue the stick straight ahead from the shoulder position and pick the far side of the net.

6. On long shots, a player can play "cat and mouse" with the goalie — create a faking action to get a reaction from the goalie. A shooter should always be thinking ahead of the goalie or trying to anticipate what the goalie is thinking.

It is important for players to remember where they took their last shot and use this information to set up the goalie on their next shot with fakes and shooting motions. For example, if a shooter scored on a long,

Diagram 14

New near side, new far side of net

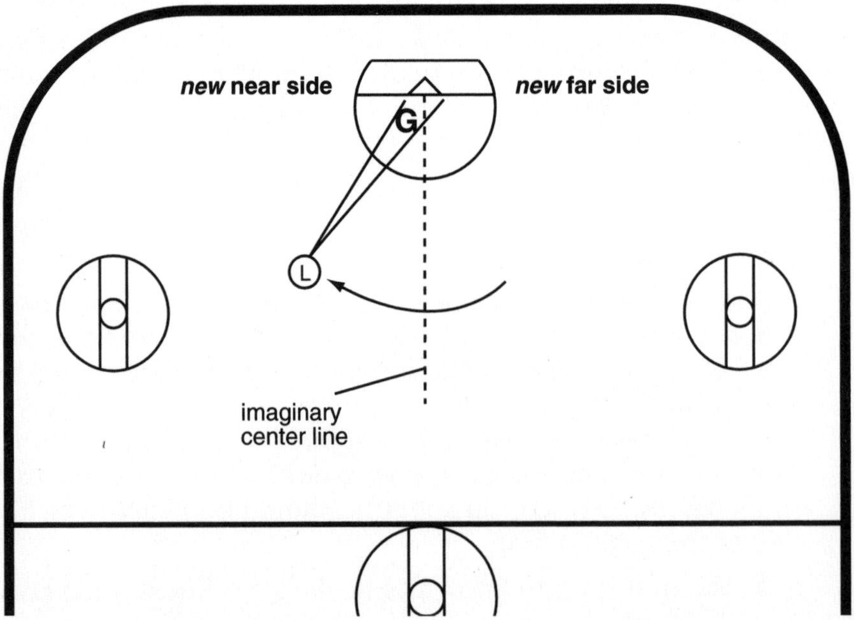

new near side   new far side

G

L

imaginary center line

short-side shot, the goalie thinks he will try it again. However, this time, before shooting, the shooter either hesitates a split-second with his stick and drops his shoulder slightly, making the goalie think he is going to shoot again for the short side, or stick-fakes to the short side. As the goalie moves across to cover the short side, the shooter continues his stick straight ahead for the long side.

7. Even though some goalies, especially reflex goalies, like to give the short side, when the overhand long-ball shooter cuts across the top, he should still look to shoot for the far top corner of the net most of the time.

8. Versus angle goalies, great shooters don't get fancy, don't fake; they just pick and shoot.

   • If they see no openings in the top corners of the net, they bounce.

   • If they see no openings on the far side first, they look to shoot near side.

   • If they have a shot straight on with the goalie, they try to step into the middle slightly to move the goalie sideways away form the near goal post.

   • If they are cutting across the top, they look for the far top corner or mid-post area, but if they can't see anything, they look to shoot a bounce shot inside the near corner post.

9. Great shooters

   • know they can shoot faster than a goalie can move.

   • feel the hardest shots are the ones they swing easy with. They do not try to swing or force the shot too hard.

   • know they can hit the open spot they are shooting at. They know accuracy is more important than hardness.

   • make sure a high percentage of their shots are bounce.

   • look at the whole net on the shot and "pick" the open spot. They do not look directly at the spot they are shooting at, called "telegraphing." Some players look at one corner and shoot to the other corner because they feel the goalies watch their eyes.

REMEMBER: Most shooters can shoot faster than a goalie can move! On long shots, stress picking a spot and shooting. Sidearm shooters, when cutting across should also look to shoot for the far top corner. The top corner short side is a very difficult shot for a sidearm shooter. A lot of times, what a shooter's eyes do not see, his stick's head can "see," especially if the stick is held high above the head or out to the side of the body.

10. Players should shoot from their "Prime Scoring Area" 90 percent of the time. But sometimes a players is caught in a situation where he is on his wrong side of the floor with the ball. If he is still in the "Secondary Scoring Area," he should shoot the ball if he has an opening, or thinks he can set up the goalie *(see Diagram 12 on p. 90).*

Once a player passes the imaginary center line, the most natural spot to shoot at is the new far side of the net (i.e., shooting across both the shooter's body and the goalie's body). A goalie will often give this new far side to a player shooting from his wrong side. A slight shoulder drop will give the goalie the impression the shooter is going to shoot to the new far side, and he may move across to cover the new far side. At this time, the shooter comes straight through with his stick and puts the ball into the new short side *(see Diagram 14 on p.112).*

Note   *It is better for younger players to hang on to the ball once they have passed the imaginary center line rather than shooting, and re-set the offense working for a better shot.*

11. Some shooters like to hide the stick from the goalie. This is done by turning the body and holding the stick behind the shoulder to block its view. They believe the goalie is like a batter in baseball: the later a batter sees the ball coming at him, the harder it is for him to hit it. Without seeing the ball a shooter might get a goalie guessing where he might place his shot and that's what a shooter wants.

REMEMBER: In shooting there is always room for improvement; no one can score 100 percent of the time. Even so, players must have the confidence they will score most of the time.

III. Practicing to Be a Shooter

A. Practice

Players must practice shooting on their own. The three keys to becoming a great shooter are practice, practice, practice! Most shooters are made through practice. Some shooters are "natural" goal scorers, yet they still have to practice. Confidence with the stick results from repetition of shots in an arena or against a wall (100–200 shots a day), and shooting at specific targets, such as nails or spots on the wall.

B. The Stick

A good carpenter cannot do a good job unless he has the right tools and looks after them. Similarly, a good lacrosse player cannot become a great shooter unless he looks after his stick. It is very important to work with one's stick at all times to make sure it is shooting right. A player should always be adjusting and playing with shooting strings, netting, and runners, but only when he can't get a feel for his stick or the flight of the ball isn't right *(see p. 16-20)*.

There are three philosophies of fixing a stick that "hooks" during a game *(see p. 37)*:

1. Most players do stick maintenance before a practice or before a game to get it working right. In a game, if a player knows his stick is "hooking" or shooting off, he can adapt by adjusting his release of the ball, but at least he will know what it is doing wrong and how to compensate. If he changes the stick during the game, he will not know what the stick is going to do.

2. Other players feel a player should never use his stick in a game if it is "hooking." If a player has to compensate for a "hook" in his stick by changing his mechanics, he will be in trouble. A player must repair the stick either during the game or between periods where adjustment can be made and the stick practiced with before going back into the game. Another possibility is to have a backup stick already broken in on the bench to use until the player's number one stick is fixed.

3. Some players make the adjustment during the game by fixing the shooting string or netting on the spot. They check the release by holding the stick in a horizontal position and pulling the stick towards themselves, spinning the ball out of the pocket to see if it rolls out properly.

> **Note** *Many great shooters know how to take a stick apart and restring it. Players who have a great love for the game take the time to find out how the tool they use works.*

C. Imaginary Shooting

1. Practice shooting with no ball and eyes closed.
2. Practice shooting with a ball with eyes closed. Memorize the "feel" of the ball in the stick as you shoot.

3. Practice shooting, concentrating on the "feel" of a good shot rather than on the target. Shooting is muscle memory and eye-hand coordination. Coaches want players to develop the proper "feeling" of shooting.

D. Shooting Progression

1. Develop good form first.
2. Develop accuracy next. Placement of the shot is more important than power in a shot. If the shot is released and correctly placed, no goalie will stop it. Work on consistency through repetition.
3. Work on speed or power third. Too much emphasis is put on power when a combination of power and accuracy is needed.
4. Work on seeing the whole net, yet concentrating on the target.
5. Finally, work on deception and faking.

E. Actual Practicing at an Empty Net

1. The most important thing when practicing shooting into an empty net is scoring — hitting the spot one aims for. This positive reinforcement of scoring gives the player a good feeling and tremendous confidence from seeing the ball being retained by the netting and hearing the "thud" on the twine.
2. The shooter should place an "X" on the floor where he likes to shoot from.
3. A player should pick only one corner of the net and shoot at it until he can hit it consistently. Practicing this way tells the player that first, his stick is working properly, and second, that he can hit what he is aiming at. Being satisfied the ball is going where he wants it to go gives a player the confidence that if a goalie gives him that opening in a game, he can score. Then, the player progresses to shooting at another corner.
4. Players must practice the type of shots they will take in a game. Try to stay within one's own abilities whether it is faking, shooting long, or shooting close in. If he tries something different, especially in a game, he will most likely botch it.
5. Practice his shot at game speed and with game moves.
6. When practicing, don't make the same mistake twice in a row. For example, a player aiming for the top corner should not miss it two times in a row without making a mental adjustment. If he shoots high the first time, he should adjust his shot so that he either hits the corner or at least his shot is lower.

7. When practicing, keep a record of the number of shots taken and scored. A good game shooting objective is 20% (i.e., score 1 out of 5 shots attempted), but in a practice shooting against a goalie, the objective should be slightly higher (40%, or 2 out of 5); shooting against the shooting board or an empty net, the objective should be 60%, or 3 out of 5.

8. When correcting the player's shot, coaches should use the "simple and straight" principle and go back to the basics.

    a. Check when "cocking" the stick that the butt points at the target, and the stick is held horizontally over the stick shoulder.

    b. Check on the follow-through that the butt of the stick ends up touching the top-hand arm elbow and the head of the stick ends up pointing at the target.

    Note *Sometimes the best helper in correcting players' shots is their own goalie because he sees his teammates shoot more than anyone.*

F. Problems in Shooting

If you can make shots in a practice, why aren't you making them in a game? Possible answers:

- You don't believe in yourself.
- You telegraph your shot. You are looking directly at where you are going to shoot.
- You take bad shots — bad angle, wrong side of the floor, being pressures defensively, screened shots.
- You rush your shots (hurry) — discipline, if not a good shot don't shoot.
- You bomb your shots — just winding up and shooting at no particular spot.
- You lack concentration; do not focus on the open spot.

IV. Types of Long Shots

A. Straight Overhand Long Shot

Here, the ball comes at a downward trajectory at the goalie, giving the shoot-

The Long Side Arm Shot

Photo 41: Cocked position

Photo 41: Release of ball

Photo 43: Follow-through

The Long Underhand Shot

*Photo 44:
Cocked position*

*Photo 45:
Release of ball*

*Photo 46:
Follow-through*

er many targets — top corners, sides, bottom corners — to aim at. The overhand shooter also has the option of releasing the ball early for a straight shot, or releasing it late for a bounce shot.

B. Overhand Long Bounce Shot

This is a very deceptive shot for a goalie because the ball comes down then goes up. There are different levels of bounce shots: the short bounce hits the floor close to the feet and to the side deflecting up around the ankles; the medium bounce hits the floor about one to two feet (0.3–0.5 m) out and to the side of the goalie ricocheting up around the goalie's hip area; the long bounce hits the floor at the top of the crease area, ricocheting into the top corner. Basically, the farther out the ball hits the floor from the goal line, the higher it goes. A player must be sure to pick a corner when using a bounce shot. Just to bounce the ball toward the net can be the most ineffective and easiest shot for a goalie to stop, resulting in a fast-break situation.

It is easier to hit the far side of the net with a bounce shot. The short-side bouncer is more difficult but if executed correctly is very deceptive.

C. Straight Long Sidearm Shot *(See Photos 41–43, p.118)*

The player slides the top hand down beside the bottom hand to get a better whip action with his stick. In fact, a sidearm shooter's hands do not move much whether passing or shooting. He starts the shot with the head of the stick at waist level, and because he usually has deeper pockets he brings his stick back farther behind his body to get more "whip" into his shot.

The sidearm shot can be very deceptive because the stick extends three feet/one metre from the body. With his arms fully extended to the side, the shooter has the advantage of aiming for the far side of the net or around the goalie. Depending on the release, the ball can go up, level, or down, but usually the ball is released on a level trajectory.

On the follow-through the stick comes around the body like a baseball swing, so with a late release the player has the option of bringing his shot back to the short side of the net, which is a very tough shot to make.

D. Straight Long Underhand Shot *(See Photos 44–46, p. 119)*

The player starts this shot with the head of the stick near the level of the floor. Again, the player slides the top hand up beside the bottom hand to create the action. The underhand shot can also be deceptive because usually the shot is low and parallel to the floor, but the follow-through is like a golf swing, and with a late release the player can make the ball rise to the top corners. This is a hard shot for a goalie to judge and stop.

V. Close-In Shots

A player who plays around the crease area grips the stick differently than the long-ball shooter. The top hand grips the stick fairly tight with the fingers, while the bottom hand holds the stick loosely so that the stick can rotate easily with all the faking. This grip allows for an increased range of motion while stick-handling close in. The creaseman relies heavily on his finesse, fluidity, accuracy, speed, and in his ability to manipulate the goalie around the net. With close-in shooting, a player does not need power as much as accuracy and quickness of shot. Therefore, he does not need to cock his stick or step into his shot.

The shooter has two main options when close-in on the goalie: he can pick and shoot for the open spot, or he can stick-fake the goalie, trying to get him to react.

No matter what a player does around the net, he must have a plan for how to beat the goalie. Therefore, he tries to set the goalie up versus the goalie trying to set him up.

A. Close-In Straight Shot Strategies

1. A player does not stick-fake close to the net because usually there's no time — he's expecting a hit from a defender, or the goalie may be out of position for a split second, or there is an opening and he just shoots for it. A player who is close-in to the net must work on getting his shot away quickly.

2. When they are close-in, some players feel it is better to catch the ball in the middle of the pocket rather than the tip because it is easier to place the ball and it is quicker to get a shot away.

3. A player must keep his stick in close to his body because when around the net the defender is close, ready to check his stick or his body. But whenever the defender is not a defensive threat, the stick can be extended from the body to move around, over, or under the goalie or to quick-stick a bad pass.

4. The head of the stick moves more quickly than the goalie and gives a player a three-foot advantage. So a player should have in his repertoire a strategy of two moves: moving the stick from an inside-out position (i.e., from vertical to a horizontal position), and moving the stick from an outside-in position (horizontal to vertical). Players should mix up these stick moves so that goalies cannot categorize them.

5. Shooting to the far side (the goalie's long side):
    •   A player can set the goalie up for a far-side shot by keeping his hands and stick in an overhand position, in close to the

body to begin with, then at the last possible moment before shooting extending his arms and moving his stick out in a sidearm position and putting the ball into the far corner. The player should avoid showing the sidearm shot until the last second.

- If the situation permits, some players extend the stick out as far as they can and put the ball in the far side, or they take a big step in front of the net. That step, plus the reach of the arms and the stick itself, gives the player extra distance to shoot around the goalie.

- A player must out-think and "out-quick" goalies that rely heavily on angles. Because they have slow lateral movement, the shooter should come around the goalie on his shot as both he and his stick can move more quickly laterally. He can reach around the goalie with his stick or take one step out in front of the net and shoot around him.

REMEMBER: A player should start with the stick close to the body, so when shooting he can reach over or around the goalie. Especially against large goalies, it is even better to run across in front of the net any time a player can, rather than running down the side of the net.

- Cutting across the top going from the near side to the far side of the net gives a player more shooting options. It also takes away the large goalie's asset of playing angles and works on the goalie's liability — his inability to move laterally quickly.

Note *Too many players reduce their scoring opportunity by running down the side of the net.*

6. Shooting for the near side (the goalie's short side):
   - A player can start with his stick in close to his body and if he sees an opening, he shoots from this position.
   - He can make the goalie think he is shooting to the far side by holding the stick out from his body, either in an overhand or sidearm position, then quickly and in one continuous motion bring it back in close to his body to take an overhand shot to the near side.
   - He can step with his inside foot (i.e., left foot or back foot) for a left-hand shot out in front of the net with his stick held out to the side and hesitate a shot to the far side (not a fake) to

move the goalie or at least "freeze" him, then bring his stick back to the near side. A slight hesitation makes all the difference close-in. Patience is a very difficult skill to teach. If the goalie moves to the far side, fluidity and speed are essential in shooting back to the near side.

Variation: The player can shoot off the wrong foot (i.e., his right foot or front foot). This is a surprise move as the back foot does not come through on the shot. The player then hesitates on his shot to the far side, not breaking his wrists, and comes back to the near side.

7. The quick-stick shot occurs when the shooter at the side of the net is wide open from a crease-to-crease pass or from a cross-floor diagonal pass.

8. Another quick-stick move is to keep the stick above the head with the arms extended upwards — this could be a result of receiving a high pass — and shooting down without bringing the stick back. This shot surprises the goalie, who expects the stick to be brought back.

9. Shooting options for a crease player are:
    *   far top corner
    *   near top corner
    *   low around the ankles (far side or near side, straight shot or bounce)
    *   under the glove hand
    *   medium shot around the hips (far side or near side, straight shot or bounce shot to the hips)
    *   between the legs — these shots work best against goalies who have a tendency to lift their sticks. But usually this shot is a "cop out" for shooters, who just throw the ball low between the legs and hope for the best because of defensive pressure, or because of lack of imagination or concentration.

10. Most players have a natural tendency to shoot for the far side of the net, but they should be aware of where the glove-hand side of the goalie is. Shooting under the glove hand — whether a bounce or straight shot — is a very good strategy requiring the goalie to make a difficult stick or leg save.

11. Some players like to shoot low most times around the hip (because of poor lateral movement of the goalie), thereby exaggerating their follow-through to make sure the ball goes low. Players aim low, so even if the goalie gets a piece of the ball it could still go in. In fact, some players try to ricochet shots off the goalie. By shooting low to the hips, they can

only miss the net one way — to the side. Whereas if a player shoots for the top corner he has two possible ways to miss the net: over the top and to the side.

12. Don't think "shot," think "score." Just pick a spot. The player can shoot off the goalie or shoot at the net, concentrating on a spot.

13. When most players get a breakaway, they usually shoot close-in. Most goalies expect at least one fake in this type of situation. This is all the more reason for the shooter just to pick a spot and shoot.

Photos 47–48: Fake to the near side (overhand)...

...and shoot to the far side (sidearm).

B. Close-in Fake-Shot or Stick-Fake Strategies

1. All players should have a patented move — their best shot, their favorite corner — that they can always depend on under pressure. Although they should use the move they feel most confident with most of the time, they should mix up their fakes, since good goalies categorize shooters by favorite fake, favorite spot, and favorite side.

    The shooter should remember what stick-fake he used last and if the goalie stopped or came close to stopping the shot. If the goalie did this, the shooter should set up the goalie the next time.

2. Some players, expecially beginners, fake their shot at the goalie, in which case the goalie will definitely not move. Players have to learn to fake at corners to get a reaction from a goalie.

3. From a hard overhand

    • stick-fake to the near side of the net back into an overhand shot to the near side;

    • stick-fake to the near side of the net back into an overhand shot to the far side;

    • stick-fake to the far side of the net back into an overhand shot to the near side;

    • stick-fake to the far side of the net back into an overhand shot to the far side; or

    • stick-fake to the near side into a fluid sidearm shot to the far side. *(See Photos 47, 48.)*

4. From a hard sidearm, stick-fake to the far side into a fluid, quick overhand shot to the near side. The far-side sidearm stick-fake greatly influences the goalie who knows that a sidearm shot can, in most cases, only go to the long side of the net; therefore, he leaves more room on the short side in anticipation of a far-side sidearm shot. The shooter then brings the stick back quickly to the near side. *(See Photos 49, 50.)*

5. From a hard sidearm, stick-fake to the far side back into a sidearm shot to the far side.

6. There are "standard fakes," but sometimes these are called "automatics" if done without thinking or "reading" what the goalie does on the fake. The ability to judge whether or not a goalie has moved for a stick-fake requires patience, experience, and a split-second response.

    a. Generally, if the goalie reacts to the stick-fake at one corner, then the shooter shoots at the opposite corner:

- The shooter looks and stick-fakes at the far top corner. If the goalie reacts, he then brings his stick back and shoots to the near side, low, waist high, or to the top corner.

Note   *The goalie knows the shooter wants to shoot to the far side (the most natural side), so for the shooter to fake to the far side and then come back to the near side can be very deceptive.*

Photos 49, 50: Fake to the far side (sidearm) ...

... and shoot to the near side (overhand).

- The shooter looks and stick-fakes at the near corner (goalie's short side). If the goalie reacts, he then reaches around him and shoots to the far corner.

- The shooter stick-fakes high. If the goalie reacts by raising the upper body or stick, he then shoots low.

b. If the goalie does not react to the stick-fake at a corner, then the shooter shoots at the same corner at which he just faked:

- The shooter looks and stick-fakes at the far corner. If the goalie does not react, he shoots at the far corner.

- The shooter looks and stick-fakes at the near corner. If the goalie does not react, he shoots at the near corner.

- The shooter stick-fakes high. If the goalie does not react, he shoots high.

7. Some players like to use two stick-fakes, but they must assess the situation to see if they have time. Don't stick-fake twice just for the sake of faking twice; have a reason for stick-faking, primarily to get a reaction from the goalie. Don't be predictable — be deceptive.

a. The close-in shooter looks at the corner he is not going to shoot at, stick-fakes once at that corner, then stick-fakes a second time at that corner, then comes back and puts the ball in the other corner.

b. The close-in shooter looks at the corner he is going to shoot at, stick-fakes at that corner, then stick-fakes at the other corner, then comes back to the original corner he faked at and puts the ball in.

c. The close-in shooter stick-fakes to the near side, then fakes to the far side and brings the ball back to the near side.

d. The close-in shooter stick-fakes to the far side, then stick-fakes to the near side and shoots for the far side.

C. Behind-the-Back Shot, or Over-the-Shoulder Shot
(See Photos 51, 52)

This shot can be used when the goalie comes with the shooter across the net and takes away the opening on the shooter's stick side (long side), leaving the side vacant that the shooter just came from (short side). Once he has passed the mid-point of the net and sees he has nothing to shoot at, the shooter thinks of this shot.

By moving the stick out to the side and slightly behind his body, the player flexes his top-hand arm, bringing his stick over his shoulder and behind his back.

For the average player, this shot is really one of desperation where there is no time on the "shot clock." If the shot clock has time left, often it is better just to keep control of the ball for a higher percentage shot. The behind-the-back shot is a "hope" shot unless a player practices it a lot.

Over-the-Shoulder Shot

Photos 51, 52: Move stick behind body, ...

...flex top-hand arm.

VI. Shooting Drills

A. Visualization

The player imagines the perfect shot and mentally sees the ball go into the net.

B. Form Shooting

The player shoots an imaginary ball while the coach gives feedback regarding his form. Then the player shoots with a ball against the boards, and coach gives feedback.

C. "Shooting Board" Drills

These drills use a shooting board, which is a 4 foot x 4 foot (1.22 m x 1.22 m) board cut out diagonally at the corners, leaving gaps for players to shoot at. The corners in the beginning should be cut out fairly large so the players can score easily, gaining lots of confidence. The players must also take a high repetition of shots to help acquire this confidence.

1. The coach uses the board to teach shooting. The player stands where he likes to shoot from and receives cross-floor passes from his partner, then shoots at the cut-out corners.

2. Once players have some confidence, the shooting board can be used to improve their shots by putting some pressure on them as they shoot at the board. Some ways of doing this:

   a. Charting all players to see what their shooting percentage is. A player should average 60% or 15–25 shots. Keep a "ladder" for the team, with the highest shooting percentage player at the top.

   b. Seeing how many goals a player can get in a row. Chart the results to create healthy competition on the team, or use money as an incentive: if a player scores 2 in a row, he gets 2 dollars; if a player scores 3 in a row, he gets 5 dollars; if a player scores 4 in a row, he gets 20 dollars; or a player can't leave practice until he scores 2 in a row.

   c. Charting the number of goals a player can score in 30 seconds, or 60 seconds.

3. The player shoots on the move. Two passers pass to the shooter for one minute. The shooter must be in constant motion so the drill also becomes a conditioner.

4. Practicing out-of-range shooting requires players to shoot out farther than they normally would.

D. Warm-Up Shooting Drill

Players with a ball form two lines. In rapid succession all the players in one line make an offensive move, around a cone placed just inside the Prime Scoring Area boundary line at about the 15-foot (4.5-m) mark, then shoot at the goalie (see Diagram 12, p.90).

1. Outside fake and cut across the top for a shot.
2. Inside fake and cut to boards and in for a shot.
3. Stutter step to a fake and a shot.
4. Fake shot and cut across the top for a shot.
5. Inside pivot and cut across the top for a shot.
6. Outside pivot and cut to boards and in for a shot.

E. Semi-circle Drill

Players with a ball form three semi-circular groups about 15 feet (4.5 m) from the crease. Players in the first line shoot in succession around the horn, then the players in the second and third line do the same thing. The next time, the players shoot alternating from side to side in the semi-circle. Lastly, the players shoot around a token screen. Coaches can vary the tempo of the drill so that players can shoot in rapid fire or in a controlled manner.

F. Breakaway Drill

The team forms a single line at center floor. The team runs in units of five players, known as lines, down the middle of the floor. If anybody on the line scores, the whole line yells out "One!" "Two!" and so on. Again, the coach can control the tempo of the drill with either

*   rapid fire shooting where there is no pause between shots, or
*   controlled shooting where there is more time between shots.

G. Follow-the-Leader Drill

Teams form a single line at the center floor. Line units run in single file following the front player who is the leader. He can vary where the shots are taken from, either cutting across the top, down the side, or down the middle. Lines compete against each other for most goals scored.

H. Two-Line, No-Pass, Cornerman Shooting Drill
(See Diagram 15)

The coach puts a cone in the middle of the floor, about 15 feet (4.5 m) from the crease. All the left shots carry a ball and take long shots after cutting

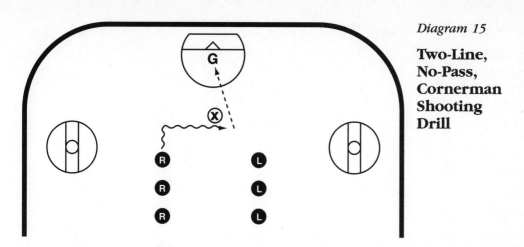

Diagram 15

**Two-Line,
No-Pass,
Cornerman
Shooting
Drill**

around the cone, then all the right-shots go. Players can shoot planted around the cone, or shoot just past the cone on the run, cutting across the top.

   Variation:Alternate the lines with left-shots, then right-shots. Make the drill into a game, rights versus lefts. Use two cones to the side of the floor (in the Prime Scoring Area) rather than in the middle. These shooting drills should be competitive and highly repetitive.

I. Two-Line, No-Pass, Creaseman Shooting Drill
   (See Diagram 16)

The coach puts the cone at the top of the crease. A left-handed ballcarrier comes out of the corner position shooting past the cone and not before, then a right-handed ballcarrier does the same thing. The lines alternate until the coach stops the drill. This is a reaction (reflexive) drill for the players and the goalie, therefore players cannot fake, but just shoot. The left-hand players stay

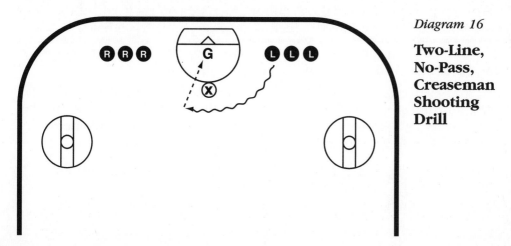

Diagram 16

**Two-Line,
No-Pass,
Creaseman
Shooting
Drill**

Diagram 17

Two-Line, Pass, Cornerman Shooting Drill

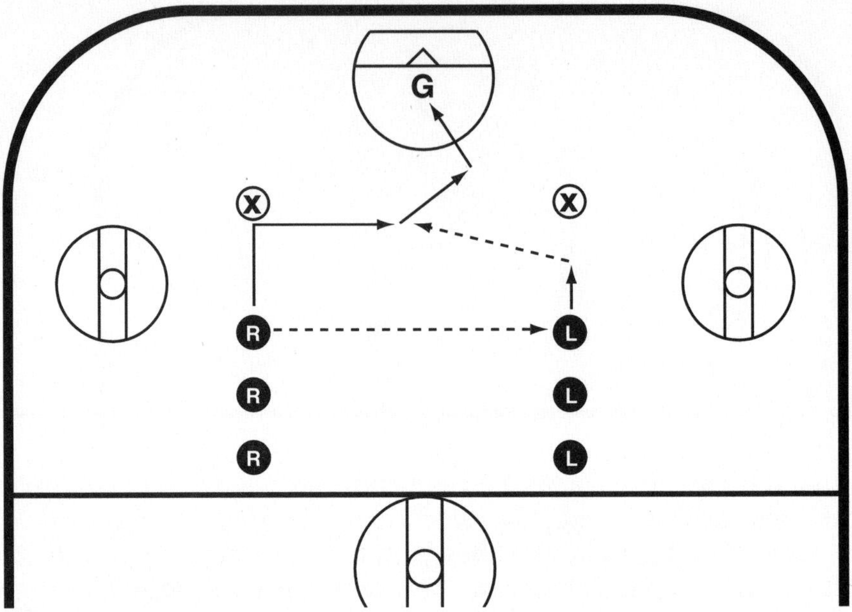

to the inside and the right-hand players stay to the outside so the players don't run into each other.

Variation: The drill is run in a more controlled manner, with the players allowed one fake. Players alternate still, but they shoot before the cone, which makes it very difficult for the goalie, since he has to move laterally quite a distance.

J. Two-Line, Pass, Cornerman Shooting Drill
(See Diagram 17)

The coach puts two cones in the Prime Scoring Area on each side of the floor. Players work on their give-and-go technique. Everybody has a ball.

1. The first player in one line throws a cross-floor pass to the first player in the other line who has put his ball down beside himself.

2. The passer then puts an offensive move on the cone and cuts to the ball for a return pass and shot. The cutter yells "Ball!" The passer must hit the cutter early enough so he has lots of time to make a good judgment in his shot; therefore, the passer's rule is, "Pass early, not late."

3. Then, the former passer picks up his ball and passes to the next player in the opposite line so he can work on his "give-and-go."

4. The players alternate from side to side until the coach stops the drill.

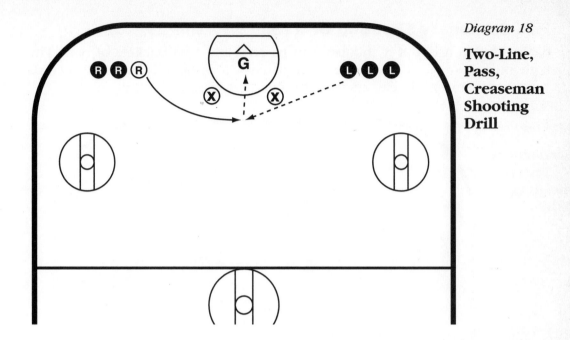

Diagram 18

**Two-Line,
Pass,
Creaseman
Shooting
Drill**

Variation: Players work on their "Go" move. There is no pass before they cut; they just cut to the ball.

K. Two-Line, Pass, Creaseman Shooting Drill
  (See Diagram 18)

This is similar to the above "Go" drill, except the players run out of the corner area. Make this drill short since the goalie has to move back and forth very quickly. The shooter must shoot between the two cones in front of the crease.

L. Merry-Go-Round Drill

This is a two-line passing drill, but the left-shots shoot continuously with the right-shots just feeding the cutters. Then the players reverse roles; the cutters learn to move without the ball, cut quickly and hard, and cut with their sticks ready to catch and shoot. The two lines can compete against each other on who scores the most goals, or on who has the best shooting percentage (number of goals to number of shots).

M. Stationary Shooting Drill *(See Diagrams 19, 20)*

This drill consists of a shooter, two passers, and two buckets of balls. The shooter shoots for one minute from his favorite spot and the coach records the number of goals. Passers feed the shooter as fast as they can.

Diagram 19

**Cornerman
Stationary
Shooting
Drill**

Diagram 20

**Creaseman
Stationary
Shooting
Drill**

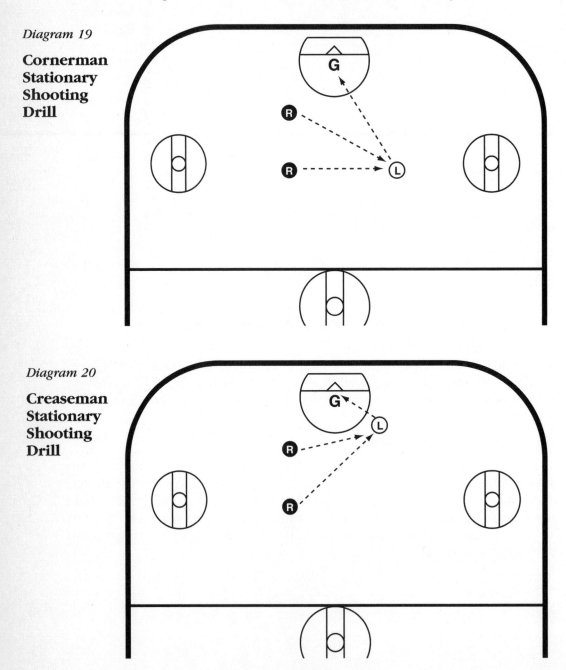

N. On-the-Move Shooting Drill *(See Diagrams 21, 22)*

Same as above, except the shooter moves from the middle of the floor to the side of the floor, or moves up and down the same side of the floor.

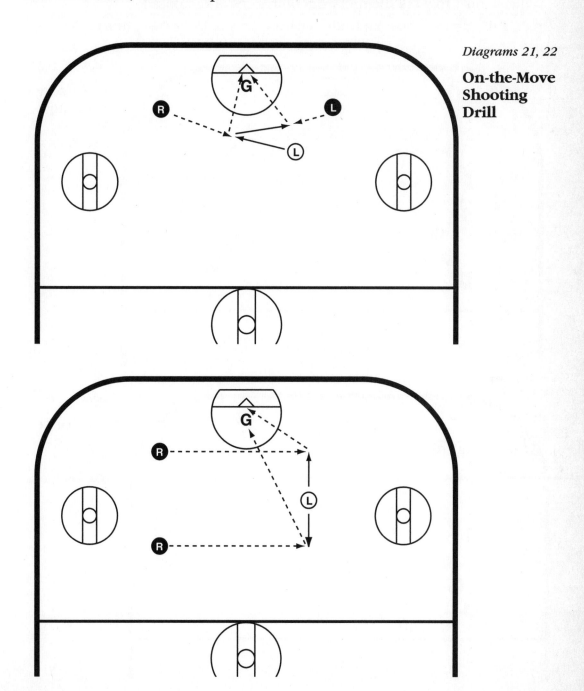

Diagrams 21, 22

On-the-Move Shooting Drill

O. Four-Corner Shooting Drill

1. Ball Starts All Shooting Drills in Top Area of Floor *(See Diagrams 23–27)*
(Remember to work the drill from both sides of the floor.)

2. Ball Starts All Shooting Drills in Crease Area of Floor *(Diagrams 28–32)*

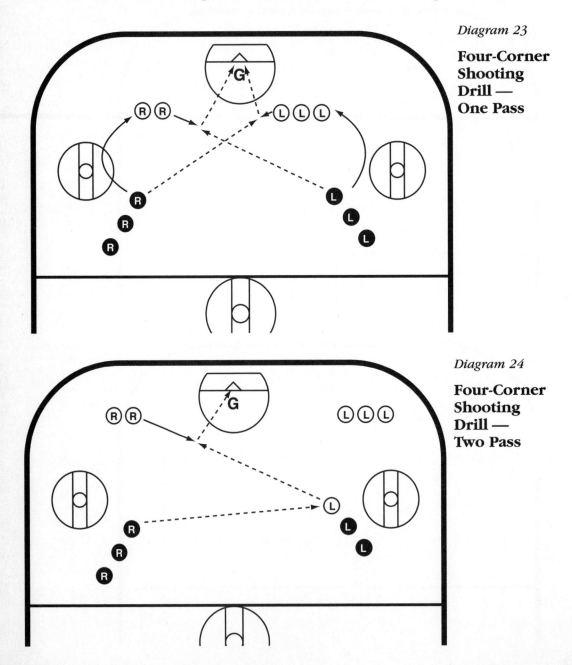

Diagram 23

Four-Corner Shooting Drill — One Pass

Diagram 24

Four-Corner Shooting Drill — Two Pass

Diagram 25

Four-Corner Shooting Drill — Three Pass

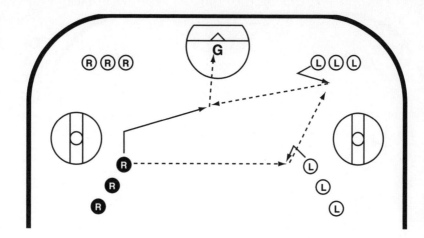

Diagram 26

Four-Corner Shooting Drill — Four Pass

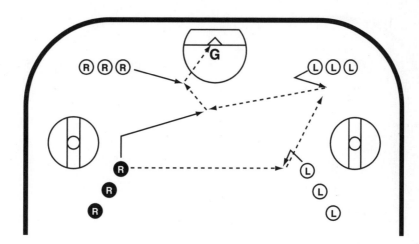

Diagram 27

Four-Corner Shooting Drill — Five Pass

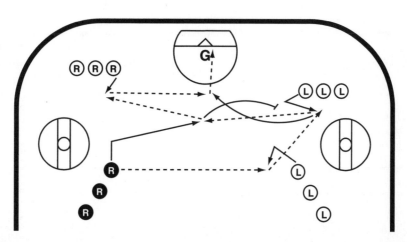

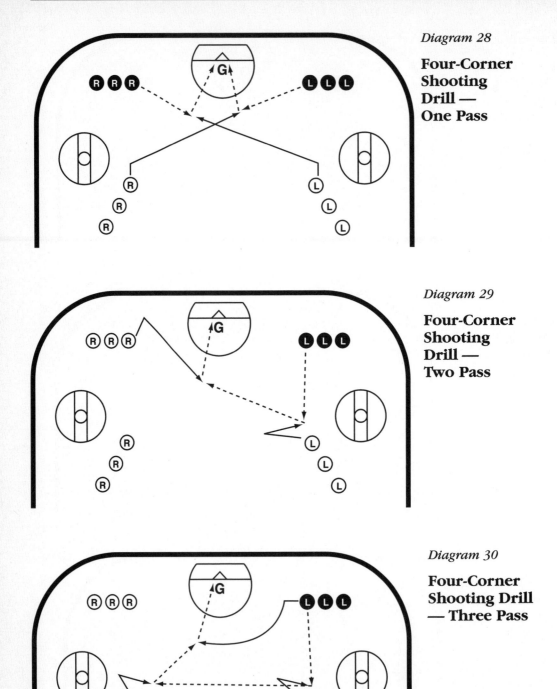

Diagram 28

Four-Corner Shooting Drill — One Pass

Diagram 29

Four-Corner Shooting Drill — Two Pass

Diagram 30

Four-Corner Shooting Drill — Three Pass

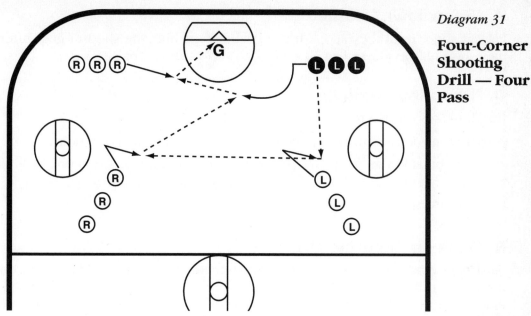

Diagram 31

Four-Corner Shooting Drill — Four Pass

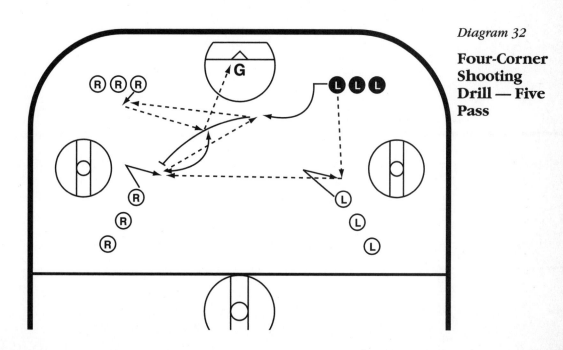

Diagram 32

Four-Corner Shooting Drill — Five Pass

P. "Showdown" Game

Players shoot until they score. If the goalie stops him, the shooter goes after the rebound. The player has 30 seconds to score three goals.

Q. "Shooting" Game

Coach makes up two teams. First team to 21 wins. Scoring:

- Score inside the imaginary semi-circle line — team gets one point.
- Score outside the imaginary semi-circle line — team gets two points.
- Score outside the imaginary semi-circle line on a bounce shot — team gets three points.

R. Close-In Shooting Drills

Most creaseman shooting drills work on speed and fluidity in faking, i.e., on the ability to keep the ball in the stick as the speed of the fake is increased. Practice both quick-stick and faking moves with or without the ball. Practice receiving a pass and incorporating a quick-stick move or fake move.

When practicing on their own, players should simulate game conditions — taking passes on the run, pretending to ward off or beat a defender, and faking/quick-sticking to all parts of the net.

— 10 —
Face-Offs

THE FACE-OFF is the process of starting play at the beginning of every period or after a goal is scored.

What follows is a basic guide to face-off rules. There may be some variation depending on which league you play under or follow. In North America, the two main lacrosse organizations responsible for setting official rules in box lacrosse are the National Lacrosse League (N.L.L.) and the Canadian Lacrosse League (C.L.A.). Consult their current rule books accordingly for more specific, up-to-date information about rules.

Two players, called centermen, place their sticks back-to-back to fight for possession of the ball by directing the ball to a teammate or by picking it up.

The ball is placed between the two sticks and the sticks must not touch the ball. The feet must be behind the center line. Once the players have assumed their positions the referee will say "set." Players taking the draw must remain motionless until the whistle is blown. Any movement after the "set" command will cause possession to go to the non-offending team.

When the referee blows the whistle the two players must draw the ball moving their sticks parallel to the center line or face-off line.

I. Face-Off Rules

Note   *The rules of the face-off are always changing from one season to the next. One time a centerman is allowed to trap, then next time the centerman has to draw straight back before he can trap, or just draw straight back with no trap. It gets very confusing, so I have tried to cover every possible type of draw in this section.*

A. There have been a number of face-off rules regarding drawing and trapping. The old rule was that a centerman could trap the ball first, then draw his stick backwards, but with the newer rules a centerman must draw his stick backwards or sideways first, then he may trap the ball. In other words, a centerman must continuously draw straight back with his stick.

> **Note** *In the N.L.L., the player must draw first, then trap or clamp, but he must keep the stick in motion and not withhold the ball from play. The player may not "dead stick" (clamp or trap and not move the stick), step on, or kick an opponent's stick. This is illegal and possession shall be awarded to the non-offending team.*

> **Note** *No matter what rule is used, a centerman cannot intentionally trap the ball down — withholding it from play — or the opposition will be awarded possession. Referees, however, will allow some trapping if the centerman does it quickly with no delay.*

B. The "open face" of the centerman's stick must face his own goal. An easy way to remember the centerman's alignment is that his right shoulder is nearest his own goal whether he is a right-shot or a left-shot centerman; his back defends his goal.

In box lacrosse, the centerman can be a right-hand shot or a left-hand shot to take the draw.

> **Note** *The face-off in the N.L.L. has the same alignment as in the field game — the draw man must be a right-handed shot. The draw man stands on the same side of the center line as the goal they are defending, facing the goal they are attacking.*

C. The referee will place the ball on the floor between the players' sticks. He will start the face-off with a whistle. The ball must not touch the sticks.

D. The centerman's feet cannot move either across the Restraining Line prior to the start of the draw or until the ball comes out of the small circle.

> **Note** *If the centerman "flinches" (moves his stick or feet before the whistle), the opposition will be awarded possession.*

E. The ball must come out of the small circle before any other players enter the large circle.

>   **Note**   *Most times the centerman in the N.L.L. will try and pick up the ball off a face-off as rules permit him protection in the face-off area from checking by the other players. Only stick-on-stick contact is allowed by the other players when reaching for a loose ball in the center circle.*

F. The centerman can only grip the shaft of the stick; he cannot touch the plastic head. He cannot move his stick prior to the whistle, and cannot trap or withhold the ball from play. He cannot lean his head over the ball. Both hands must be on the handle of the stick and touch the floor. His feet may not touch the stick.

G. No portion of either stick may touch nor may either player be in contact with his opponent's body by encroaching (infringe, trespass) into his opponent's territory. The centerman cannot touch his opponent's stick with his hands or feet.

II. Right-Handed Centerman Stance

A. The Side Stance for a Right-Handed Centerman
(See Photo 53)

This is the most common method used by a centerman for taking the face-off.

1. Body Position

The main thing in taking the stance is to be balanced and feel comfortable. Take a semi-crouch or squat position with knees bent for a quick, explosive move. Getting into this position gives one a low center of gravity which helps to maintain good balance, stability, and strength. Always stay low to the ground and be the last man up. Usually the last man to stand up wins the draw.

2. Placement of Feet

Get in a crouched position beside the stick with a side-staggered stance. The front foot is parallel with the stick while the back foot is turned sideways to give support and a solid brace to push from. Some players point both feet at the ball, i.e., in the direction they want their center of gravity to go. A right-hand centerman stands on the same side of the stick as his own net (that is, on the outside of his stick). Some players like to kneel on one knee beside their stick but this puts them at a disadvantage if they want to get up quickly.

Photo 53:
Side stance
for a right-
handed
centerman
(black
sweater).

3. Grip of Stick

The top hand moves up to the throat of the stick (without touching the plastic) while the bottom hand grabs the butt of the stick or up the shaft, no farther than the mid-point (N.L.L. rules now allow players to place their hands anywhere along the shaft).

A strong centerman can place his hands close together, giving him a smaller radius to move his stick away or towards his body, while a weaker centerman should place his hands wider apart to make up for the strength factor. The knuckles of both the top hand and the bottom hand are flat to the floor. This position of the knuckles helps the centerman to draw and trap simultaneously. The power comes from both hands when rotating the stick inwards, but the top hand is the key hand as most of the power comes from this hand.

Note   *The old rules were such that the face-off was a straight*
trap. In this case, the wrist of the top hand would be
rotated backwards (before the actual trap) so that the
back of the hand was underneath the stick and flat to
the floor for more leverage. This position of the top
hand was important because more power could come
from this hand as it had farther to rotate forward.

In this "power" grip position, the opposition player would have had difficulty moving the head of the centerman's stick. This works on the same principle as turning a doorknob: the stronger somebody wants to turn a doorknob, the farther they rotate their wrist before grabbing the doorknob so that they will have more leverage.

4. Pressure on the Stick

A centerman can put weighted pressure on the stick to help muscle the "back" of the pocket completely flush to the floor over the ball as he draws back. A centerman does this by staying low and exerting downward pressure with his body weight onto his front hand and front foot. The body's weight over the top hand helps to muscle the stick down on the trap. Some players use the knee as leverage and for more power, putting the right elbow behind their right knee.

He can start the face-off with the body weight between his hands, but as a player begins his trap, the body rolls over the top hand and stays there.

If a player can get away with it before the actual draw, he should lean the head of the stick slightly over the ball, rather than keeping it straight up and down, to give himself an advantage.

Or the centerman can keep his weight on his feet, not on his hands. He keeps his body weight on his feet, leaving his hands free to move quickly, for fast stick action.

B. Straddle Stance for a Right-Handed Centerman
(See Photo 54)

(Note: Not permitted by N.L.L.)

1. Body Position

Take a straddle position with knees bent.

Photo 54: Straddle stance for a right-handed centerman (black sweater).

2. Placement of Feet

In this position the centerman straddles the stick — the stick is between the legs and the stance is wide, while the player stays in the semi-crouched position.

Not many players use this position of standing over the top of the stick, but those centermen who do, usually lefties, say they have more power and control.

3. Grip of Stick

The top hand is placed at the throat of the stick while the bottom hand grabs the shaft half-way up.

4. Pressure on the Stick

As with the Side Stance, the centerman leans forward over the stick, almost looking straight down at the ball.

III. Face-Off Techniques

There is really no wrong way when taking a stance to take the face-off. A centerman will take the stance that he feels comfortable and natural with. He will also find the best and easiest technique to win the face-off, knowing he still might have to adjust this technique and have counters for certain opposition centermen. The secret to becoming a good centerman is to learn from the experienced centermen one faces off against.

A. The "Trap" or "Clamp" *(See Photos, 55, 56)*

In this technique the centerman does a straight draw backwards while simultaneously doing a quick forward rotation of the top-hand wrist, turning the head of the stick over flat to the floor, thereby trapping the ball, while continuously drawing the ball in front of himself to scoop it up.

The draw and trap is done in one continuous motion by the top-hand wrist. Both the top hand and the bottom hand help to pull the stick back, and both give power when turning the stick on the trap. Because the right-hander traps away from his body, he has a natural advantage of the body weight moving in the same direction as the wrist is turning. If the centerman gets his stick underneath his opponent's stick first, he will win the draw. This "trap" technique is not a finesse move, but mainly a power move. So players should just draw and trap in one continuous motion.

REMEMBER: Stay low to the ground!

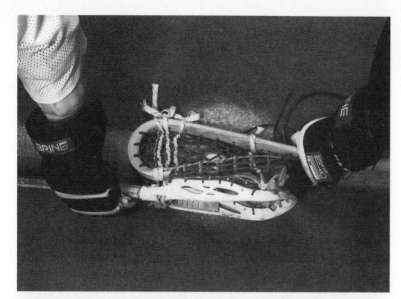

The Trap

*Photo 55:
Top hand turns
the stick over
(black sweater)*

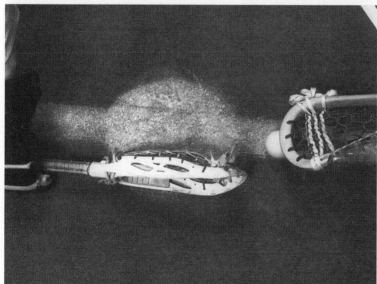

*Photo 56:
Draw the ball
in towards
you.*

Gaining the Advantage

There are a number of ways of getting the better of the opponent in a face-off. These advantages are created as the referee is placing the ball between the sticks and small adjustments made as he moves out of the circle. Counting from the time the referee leaves the small circle until he blows his whistle, may reveal a pattern in the referee's behavior, depending on where he backs out.

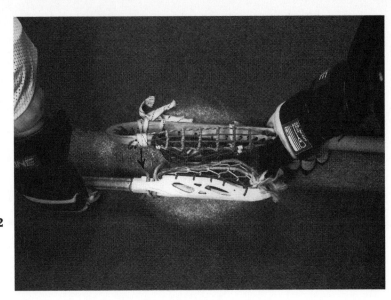

Photo 57:
**The Trap —
Advantage #2**
*Lean stick
over the ball
(black
sweater).*

So, "Cheat until you are caught."

To either gain a split-second or get more power, a centerman can try one or all of these methods:

Advantage #1

Lift the handle about 2 inches (5 cm) off the floor with the back hand to help get more body weight into the trapping motion.

Advantage #2 (Photo 57)

By leaning his stick slightly over the top of the ball, the centerman can get underneath the stick of the opposition centerman quicker and thereby trap first.

Advantage #3

Push the pocket in at the back of the stick. This will help the centerman get over the ball quicker and position the ball better.

Advantage #4 (Photo 58)

Push the stick handle away from the body with the bottom hand (about a 45-degree angle to an opponent's stick). This movement helps avoid resistance from the opponent's stick when he rotates his own stick downward. The thick end (the tip) of the head will now be in a position so that, when the centerman turns his stick to trap, the tip will go down without hitting the opponent's stick.

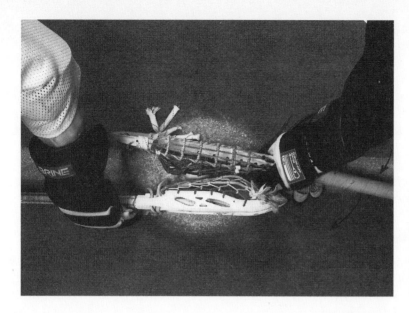

Photo 58:
**The Trap —
Advantage #4**
*Push handle
away from
body (black
sweater).*

Advantage #5 (Photo 59)
Move the stick forward slightly to get the ball to the "throat" of the stick or as close to it as possible. Besides all the power being at the throat, the stick is narrower at the throat making it quicker to go over top of the ball; in addition, this placement makes it is easier to get underneath the fatter part of the opponent's stick and blocks the opposition's view of the ball. The centerman will

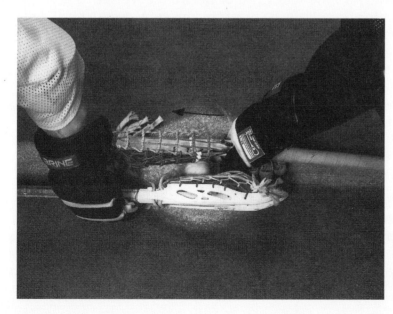

Photo 59:
**The Trap —
Advantage #5**
*Move stick for-
ward (black
sweater).*

have more netting to draw on the ball when pulling back, with the result that the ball will come out on his side of the circle.

Advantage #6
Move the top hand closer to the throat; this will give the centerman an edge by getting his glove involved in the trap, either to block his opponent's stick from turning or to use his glove as leverage to push his opponent's stick back.

Advantage #7
As you clamp with the top hand jam your thumb into the opposing player's stick so he cannot clamp.

B. The "Draw" or "Rake"

This is a quick move of pulling the stick straight back towards the body with both hands. With this drawing motion the ball is pulled by the netting in the same direction as the centerman's stick is pulled, resulting in the ball coming out on his side of the circle.

The referee tries to place the ball in the middle of the two sticks so neither player has an advantage. The trick is that the more netting a centerman can draw on, the better chance he has of winning the draw. So, just before the whistle, move the stick slightly forward to get the ball as close to the "throat" as possible (Advantage #4). This maneuver will give the centerman more netting to draw on and thereby a higher percentage of the ball popping out on his side of the circle.

Another trick is to turn the stick inwards before the whistle to prevent the opponent from getting the advantage of putting his stick over the ball, and getting underneath his stick first (Advantage #2). This will help put more pressure on the ball with the netting and the inside edge of the tip of the stick as the centerman pulls the ball back.

The "draw" is a move of quickness versus the strength of the "trap."

> **Note**   *If two centermen just draw straight back, the ball will stay in the middle of the small face-off circle. A centerman must do different things to get an edge.*

C. The "Double" Draw

Here, as the opponent draws, the centerman goes with him by moving his stick forward attempting to push the ball to the throat of his stick (Advantage #4). With the ball at or near the throat, the centerman stops his forward draw and starts to draw back because he now has more "gut," or netting to draw on. Thus, the ball pops out on his side. Also, as he moves his stick forward, he is turning it inwards (Advantage #2) to help put more force on the ball with the netting to stop it from being pulled by the opposition's netting. This maneuver works against a centerman who also likes to "draw."

D. The "Hesitation" Draw

For best results with this technique, the right-handed centerman should take a kneeling stance and align his left knee with the face-off dot or with the tip of his opposition's stick. He does this to get a subtle advantage — now he has to place his stick on the outside of his knee; as a result, the stick is slanted at an angle to his opponent's stick, which should be straight (Advantage #3). Being down on one knee may give a player less mobility, but this stance helps in setting up the "hesitation" draw because the stick is at an angle; plus, it gives the stick stability. A player may be slower to get up with one knee on the floor, but if he gains possession of the ball, he does not have to worry about getting up quickly.

The top hand is placed at the throat of the stick with all the player's body weight on it, and the bottom hand grips the stick about two-thirds of the way down for more strength. The bottom hand rests against the left knee for more stability and strength.

As the face-off starts, the centerman holds his stick straight up and down, but as the referee moves away, he turns his stick inwards a quarter turn to get an advantage (Advantage #2). Rotating the stick a quarter turn helps to put more physical pressure on the ball using the netting portion of the stick. As the opposition centerman draws back, the ball will be restrained by the netting, the shooting strings, and the tip of the centerman's stick.

The centerman lets the opposition centerman draw first, but keeps his stick still. He must be very quick and anticipate his opponent's move. As the opponent starts his draw, the centerman does not draw, but merely holds his stick, preventing the ball from being drawn back. This drawing action by the opposition centerman does not bring the ball out, because the ball is being retained by the netting, shooting strings, and tip of the centerman's stick. The ball now ends up at the tip of the opponent's stick, where he will lose strength. This is because the farther the ball gets from the middle of the netting, the less power he will have; however, the ball will still be in the middle of the centerman's netting for a powerful trap.

E. The "Flip" *(See Photos 60, 61)*

With this technique, as the centerman continuously draws back, he traps — turns the back of his stick downward, then continues to bring the stick around, knocking or flipping the ball back to his goalie with the back of his stick. From the beginning of the move to the end, he turns his stick 180

The Flip

Photos 60, 61:

Trap the ball (black sweater), ...

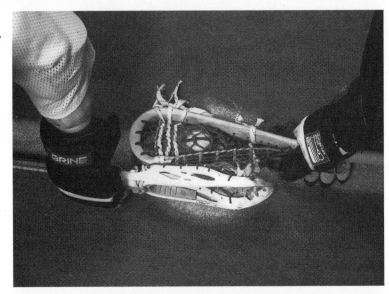

...continue to bring the stick around and knock the ball back with the "back" of the pocket (black sweater).

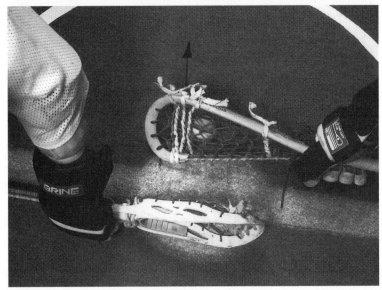

degrees. The wrist rotates forward on the trap and continues rotating around so that the wrist actually pushes the stick backwards. This "flip" move must be done quickly with no hesitation on the trap.

F. The "Up-and-Over" *(See Photos 62, 63)*

This technique is a move of split-second quickness and finesse, with the centerman going over the top of the ball, getting his stick between the opponent's stick and the ball, then knocking it back with the face of the pocket. He

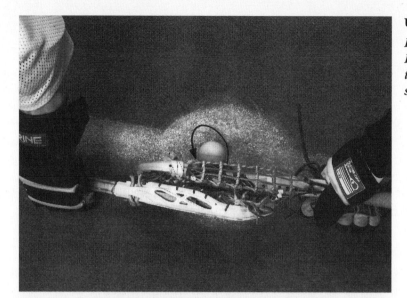

Up and Over

Photos 62, 63: Lift the stick over the ball (black sweater) ...

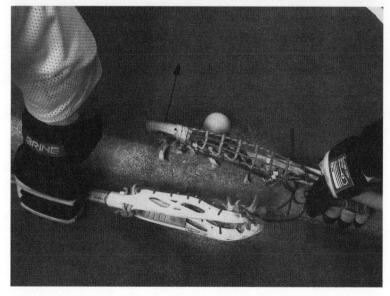

... then knock the ball back with the "front" of the pocket (black sweater).

can either lift up the throat end of his stick to bring it over the ball, or just lift the head of his stick over the ball while at the same time using the handle to block his opponent's stick from trapping. The centerman tries to use his shaft to block the opponent's stick, but in a game he usually uses his glove.

To get an advantage, he can start the face-off holding the stick's head in the air rather than resting it on the floor. Some players even wear bigger gloves to help keep the stick off the floor.

Note *Using one's shaft and jamming it into the head of the opponent's stick is a powerful move.*

Variation: This is the strength move of going up-and-over. The centerman concentrates on his opponent's stick rather than the ball at the beginning of the move. He picks up his stick and using the shaft prevents his opponent's head from trapping down. By moving his top hand forward just before the draw he can use it also to help block his opponent's stick. Here he must use all his strength to get underneath the stick of the trapping opponent. The centerman must keep digging and be persistent so he eventually will get under his opponent's stick's head and push it from the ball, letting the ball go under his own stick, then knocking it back to a teammate.

G. The "Block" *(See Photos 64, 65)*

This technique is a defensive maneuver to counter an opponent who wins by trapping. With the "Block" technique, rather than the shaft being used to block the head of the stick, the tip of the head is used to interfere with the opponent trapping down on the ball.

As the referee moves away from the face-off, the centerman pulls the butt-end of the handle towards his body, placing the head at roughly a 45-degree angle to the opponent's head, and with the tip straight up and down, pushes it in towards his opponent's stick. The stick is now in good position to block the opponent's stick as he tries to turn his stick to trap. The centerman then turns this into an offensive move by sweeping the ball out from underneath his opponent's stick.

Variation: The "sweep" technique — the centerman pulls the end of the handle towards his body, but this time he turns the stick face down on the floor, goes underneath his opponent's stick and sweeps the ball from underneath his opponent's stick with the frame of his stick. His opponent can only trap the ball into the back of his stick's pocket. This is strictly an offensive move.

IV. Left-Handed Centerman Stance

The disadvantage for most left-handed centermen is that they are natural right-handed people and the power hand is the left hand, which is their weaker hand.

A. The Side Stance for a Left-Handed Centerman

1. Body Position

Assume the same body position as a right-handed centerman.

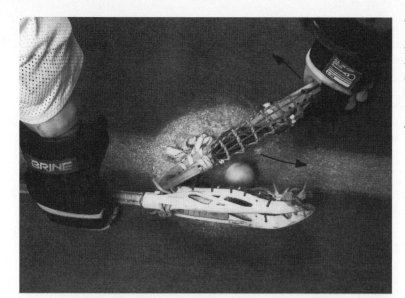

The Block

Photos 64, 65: Pull the handle towards the body (black sweater) ...

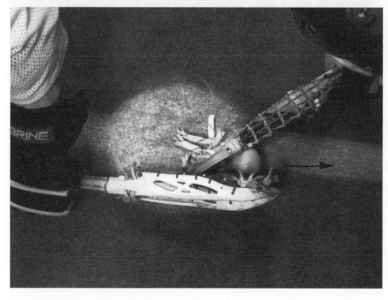

... and sweep the ball out.

2. Placement of Feet

A left-handed centerman has the same stance as a right-handed centerman but he stands on the same side of the stick as the opposition's net, i.e., on the inside of the stick.

3. Grip of Stick and Techniques

a.   For the "trap" technique, the left-handed centerman can take a normal grip with his left hand at the throat and rotate his wrist backwards turning his stick towards his body to trap. Again, he is at a disadvantage because this is his weaker hand and the rotation backwards is not a natural one.

b.   For the "draw" technique, he has the same advantage as a right-handed centerman.

c.   For the "flip" technique, he can turn his stick towards his body by rotating his top-hand wrist backwards to get the head flat to the floor. Then he continues rotating his wrist to end with the back of the wrist under the stick and pushing the stick backwards with his palm.

d.   For the "up-and-over" technique, he can pick up his stick's shaft to prevent his opponent's head from trapping down, while at the same time pushing his opponent's stick away from the ball and then knocking the ball to a teammate with the shaft or head. This is a more natural move than trying to trap the ball, and is a good move against a hard trap or a plastic stick.

e.   For all these techniques, the left-hand centerman can also take a reverse grip with the left hand, similar to the one a hockey centerman uses on a backhand face-off. This grip is becoming very common and allows more leverage and power, as a player can grip the stick on the outside with the wrist at a 45-degree angle to the floor, and on the rotation he can use not only his wrist and forearm but also his upper back for more strength. Again, the difference with this left-handed reverse grip is that the trap comes toward the body, rather than away from it as with right-handers, which compensates for the weakness of the left hand *(see photo 54, white sweater, p. 145)*.

B. Straddle Stance for a Left-Handed Centerman

(Not allowed in N.L.L.)

This stance is more commonly used by left-handers. It is the same stance as a right-hander uses except that the top hand is the left hand. The objective is to counter the power of the right-hander by using quickness and being in a better position to react to a loose ball.

V. Face-Off Tips

A.   The basic philosophy for a centerman is to do whatever he can to offset the advantage of the opposition and/or to do whatever he can to get the advantage.

Note   *Most times, whoever gets the best advantage before the
actual face-off wins. Some useful techniques in this
regard include tilting the stick inward slightly over the
ball, placing the stick at an angle to get an advantage
when trapping, putting the feet over the restraining
line to get a leverage advantage, and moving the
stick's head forward slightly to get the advantage of
having more netting to draw on.*

B.   If the opposition centerman keeps winning by taking an unfair advantage, a complaint should be made to the referee. Especially for a very
important face-off, the referee should be informed loudly — so the opposition can hear — that, for example, "his foot is over the Restraining
Line." This could get the opposition slightly distracted because now he'll
be concentrating on not putting his foot on the line rather than on the
face-off. Also, the referee might get distracted watching that the opponent does not step on the line.

   On some nights a referee will let things go and other nights another
referee will call a game tightly, so a centerman has to be smart enough to
know what he can get away with, with certain referees.

C.   Possession is the most important thing. If a centerman can win 60 percent of his face-offs with the help of his teammates, he is doing an excel-
lent job.

D.   If possible, a centerman should pick up the ball from the face-off —
"pick it up" rather than knock it to a teammate or back to his goalie.

E.   In a regular game, 80 percent of the time the centerman is trying to
knock the ball to a teammate, knock it back to his goalie, or pick it up,
but it may still go loose. The other 20 percent of the time the centerman
is trying to get the ball free from his opponent's control.

   In today's game, the art of actually winning the face-off, with the
result of the centerman picking it up, has disappeared. Most centermen
just knock the ball loose or draw it to a teammate because the opposing
players are too close and too quick getting in on the face-off circle and
hitting the centerman.

F.   On winning the face-off, the centerman's options are:

   •   to draw and trap, and scoop up the ball facing it; or

   •   to draw and trap, then knock the ball to a teammate, usually
       behind himself. He can knock it back in a sweeping motion
       with the back of his pocket, or he can knock it back with the
       tip of his stick. He can also knock the ball forward to a crease-

man towards the Offensive Zone, or he can knock it backwards to his goalie in the Defensive Zone.

When executing the trap in the Straddle Stance position,
the centerman draws, traps, and knocks the ball between his
legs. He does this so his teammates, not he, can pick it up,
although he can pursue it as a loose ball.

- To draw and trap, letting the ball go loose, then pursuing it as
  a loose ball. Just as a good centerman does not use the same
  technique every time, he does not hit the ball to the same
  spot; sometimes it is easier to go forward, sometimes it is easier to go backwards or to a certain player.

G. Some centermen feel a "trapper" will always beat a straight "draw" man,
    but it still boils down to strength, quickness, and technique.

H. Some centermen feel a right-hander has a natural advantage over a left-
    hander because his top hand is his stronger hand and his body weight is
    moving in a natural forward motion, but there are many left-handers who
    have great technique and are tough to beat.

I. A combination of good technique, quickness, and strength will win most
    of the time. So, unless a centerman has all these qualities, he needs to fig-
    ure out how to beat his opponent. A player must analyze his strengths
    and how to use them, and analyze his opponent and how to adjust to his
    opponent's strengths and weaknesses.

J. A centerman should try to do what he is most comfortable with and put
    the onus on his opponent to beat him. But he should not become pre-
    dictable.

K. If a centerman can get away with some things, he should keep doing
    them. Referees let players do what they want as long as they do it quick-
    ly, especially in tight games. If players delay the trap, they will be called
    for "withholding the ball from play."

L. Before getting into his stance, a centerman should get a mental picture
    of what his opponent did on the last face-off. If a centerman is getting
    beaten and knows what technique his opponent is going to use, he
    should use this knowledge as an edge.

- He must be ready to get a split-second jump on the opponent
  by taking an advantage position with his stick.

- He must have a counter move.

- He can try to outguess the opponent.

- He can simply copy what the opposition centerman does. If
  he cannot beat him, he copies him.

- He grabs the opponent's webbing with his top-hand fingers underneath his stick.

- He tries to keep the ball loose by leaning all his weight on the top hand and raking the ball straight back with all his strength.

- Once his opponent traps, the centerman traps over top of his opponent's stick and ball. The ball will either pop out or both players will be called for a stalemate and will be thrown out of that particular face-off.

- The "sweep" move can be used to counter the trapper.

- "Up-and-over" is also a good move to counter a trapper.

- The coach can send two centermen into the game: the first centerman will cause a stalemate by trapping the ball along with the opposition centerman. Then both of these centermen will be thrown out of the face-off. Then the second centerman comes in to take the draw.

   The draw man should always work his opponent, trying to beat him, and work the referee a little, hoping to focus attention on his opponent and off himself.

- If a centerman cannot beat a certain type of opponent, a teammate should take the face-off. It seems that certain centermen have more success against certain opposition centermen. So a player should not be so stubborn as to prevent another teammate from taking the face-off. Some nights a centerman feels he can beat anybody; then there are other nights when he just can't beat anybody. Those are the nights he should let a teammate take the face-offs.

   If the centerman has lost a draw for a violation, he should ask the referee what he did wrong at the next face-off. He should try to learn from his mistakes and what they are calling that night. A centerman gets better by analyzing and copying opposition centermen.

VI. Face-Off Alignment

Most times a centerman wants to pick up the ball off a face-off, but knocking it to a teammate might be just as advantageous depending on who is on the line (i.e., good loose-ball players), and how the opposition has lined up. When in doubt, the goalie is always open.

A. Stance of the Centerman's Teammates on the Circular Line

The centerman's teammates should keep the following in mind at face-off time:

- Be physically ready — low and crouched, with stick in "ready" position; do not stand.

- Be mentally ready and alert to charge the ball. The attitude is, "That's our ball." It's man against man. Make sure that your check does not get the ball.

  Some players' attitude is, "I'm going to pick up the ball," versus other players' attitude of, "I'm going to stop my opponent from picking up the ball." The first attitude is an offensive, aggressive attitude of playing the ball to pick it up; the second is a defensive (slower) attitude of preventing the opponent from picking it up. The former attitude makes a player more aggressive and a split-second quicker.

- Try to anticipate where the ball is coming from on the draw.

- All five players should talk beforehand and have a signal or set play where the ball will go.

B. Positioning on the Line

1. The centerman pursues the ball wherever it goes unless he picks it up, or knocks it completely back to the goalie. He must stay low to keep a low center of gravity for better balance. In pursuit of the ball he must be relentless, aggressive, and persistent — scoop the loose ball up with two hands on the stick and then protect it with his body. It is impoartant to keep the butt of the handle low to the ground for an easier scoop pickup.

2. The cornerman and pointman play on the outside, or the stick side of their opponent, or both. They interfere with the opposition's stick by putting their own over it, or interfere with the opposition's fast break from the face-off by putting their leg behind the opposition's leg. If the opposition tries to shoot in to check the centerman (not permitted in N.L.L.) or to go after a loose ball, the cornerman will interfere with him by putting his stick or body in front of the opposition's body to hold him or slow him down.

3. If the centerman knows he is going to win the face-off, he places the two defensive players on the inside of their checks to form a "cup" where he can place the ball.

   Three men should be positioned behind a face-off man who is "winning"; all three need to remember their defensive responsibilities.

If the centerman knows the opposition centerman will knock the ball back, he places one teammate opposite the opposition centerman, on the outside of his check, and the other teammate in the middle of the floor.

4. If the opposition centerman keeps winning, the centerman must line up his players a certain way to play the lost draw — in the same fashion as he would align them if he thought he was going to win the draw.

   a. The centerman makes sure one of his teammates lines up behind the opposition centerman and fires in to check the opposition centerman.

   b. If the opposition centerman keeps knocking the ball back to his goalie, a player should be positioned half-way back between the center face-off circle and the goalie's crease.

   c. If all else fails, three players should be placed back on defense to protect the goal.

5. Set plays off the face-off:

   a. The centerman hits the ball directly back to the goalie.

   b. The centerman knocks the ball directly back to a teammate. When drawing directly back to a teammate, the ball must go to the side of the teammate, who hopefully has sealed or boxed out his opponent.

   c. The centerman draws the ball directly out behind himself; either his creaseman or the cornerman will run in and pick up the ball.

   d. The centerman pushes the ball behind the opposition center-man and a teammate picks up the ball.

   e. The centerman draws, traps, and picks up the ball looking for the creaseman breaking toward the net. The creaseman can just break and beat the defender on sheer speed, or the other creaseman can set a pick on the breaking creaseman's defender.

      On this pass from the draw, the centerman stays down on the draw and even on the pickup; the pass is gone before he stands up.

6. On possession of the ball by the centerman, the two creasemen flare out to the boards looking for a quick fast-break pass. If the ball is loose from the draw, they pursue the ball on their side of the floor.

VII. Priorities for Taking a Face-Off

The essential priorities of a centerman taking a face-off are:

A. Concentration

The centerman msut shut everything out and focus on the ball, the referee's whistle, his technique, and what the opposition centerman is going to do.

B. Stance

A player should be comfortable and balanced so he can concentrate on his draw. Weight on the front hand and front foot.

C. Grip

The top-hand grip is the most important because this is where most of the power comes from.

D. Alignment of Stick

The stick is tilted inward and slanted at an angle.

E. Anticipation

The centerman must anticipate his opponent's action and the referee's whistle.

F. Combination of Strength, Quickness, and Technique

A centerman must learn to use his asset, whether it is strength or quickness, to complement his technique.

G. Intelligence

A centerman must learn to analyze the opposition centerman and figure out why he is losing or winning.

H. Competitiveness and Determination

The centerman must fight for and pursue all loose balls.

VIII. Face-Off Drills

A. One-on-One Counter Drill

Player traps, partner counters; player draws, partner counters.

B. Two on the Line Drill

Two players pursue a loose ball thrown or rolled from the face-off circle.

C. 3-on-2 from Face-Off Drill

Both centermen fight for the loose ball. Nobody touches the ball except the centermen. The centerman who gets possession runs a 3-on-2.

D. 5-on-5 Face-Off Drill

Coach stands in the face-off circle and throws the ball in different directions. Two teams react to the ball and fight for possession.

E. Draw-Clamp and Scoop Up the Ball

Stress staying low, weight on the feet, small pressure on the stick, not the gloves.

F. Draw-Clamp and Bat the Ball to the Boards

Control where you want the ball to go.

— 11 —
Goaltending

GOALTENDERS do make a difference. They can make a bad team into a good team and a good team into a championship team. Goaltenders are the backbone of the team, as they can make up for a poor defense and help to generate an offense by their quick initiation of the fast-break.

Yet, goaltenders are often neglected in practice, sometimes used merely as targets by their teammates, and are usually told by their coaches to figure out the skills of their position on their own. A remark commonly made by too many coaches is, "I don't like to work with goaltenders because I don't know much about the position. So I let them develop on their own." This chapter is intended to remedy this situation.

I. Terminology for Goaltenders

Short Side — the goalie's "short side" or the shooter's near side is the side of the net closest to the ball. (See Diagram 34 on p. 166.)

Long Side — the goalie's "long side" or the shooter's "far side" is the side of the net farthest from the ball. (See Diagram 34 on p. 166.)

Net or Goal — four feet by four feet/1.22 m by 1.22 m (4 X 4$^{1}/_{2}$ feet in the N.L.L.) — made up of two metal goal posts and a cross bar covered with a netting made of heavy string.

Floor Terminology — See Diagram 33 on next page.

Goal Line — a line from goal post to goal post. If the ball goes past this line it is a goal.

Crease — 9 feet/2.7 m radius from the center of the goal line in a semi-circle pattern. Offensive players cannot step on this line or they lose possession of the ball.

Diagram 33

Floor Terminology

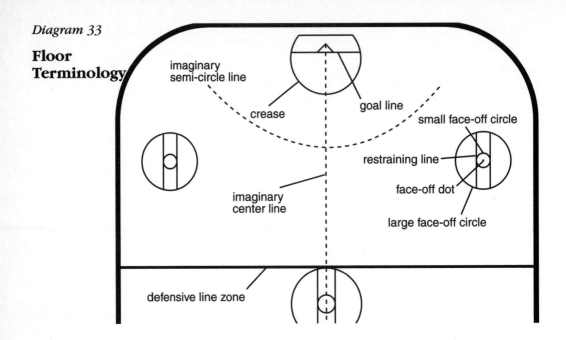

imaginary semi-circle line

crease

goal line

small face-off circle

restraining line

face-off dot

imaginary center line

large face-off circle

defensive line zone

Diagram 34

Goalie's Long Side and Short Side of the Net

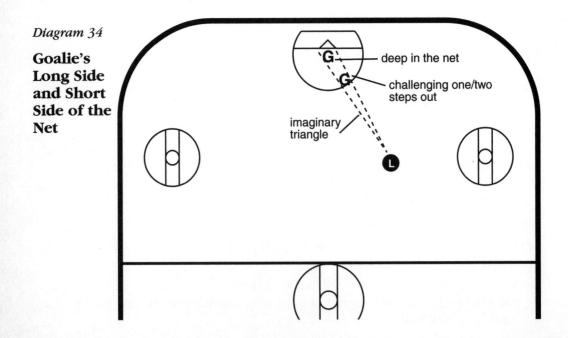

deep in the net

challenging one/two steps out

imaginary triangle

Defensive and Offensive Zone Lines— lines across the width of the arena from side board to side board to distinguish the defensive and offensive area.

Imaginary Center Line — an imaginary line down the middle of the floor, parallel to the side boards, that breaks the offensive area into ball side and off-ball side.

Imaginary Semi-Circle Line or Arc— an imaginary line 15 feet/4.6 m from the crease from which the ballcarrier becomes a threat to score.

Side Face-Off Circle — the face-off circles on the left and right side of the goalie.

II. Customizing Goaltending Equipment

The rule of thumb on equipment and protection is, if a goalie gets hurt in a certain area, fix it so that he will not get hurt there again. But it is more important to protect all areas of the body before the goalie gets hurt; as the saying goes, "Better safe than sorry."

Goalies can get welts and bruises on the arms, legs, shoulders, toes and thumbs, so be certain these areas are well protected. Make sure the equipment fits comfortably and is both protective and flexible.

A. Ice Hockey Goalie Jock

Pad with a sponge or towel behind the cup for extra protection.

B. Ice Hockey Pants

To protect the thighs, put compressed foam behind the thigh fibers in the pants to absorb the impact of the shots. In the inner thigh and crotch area of the pants, sew in pockets on the inside of the pants from top to bottom and stuff these pockets with compressed foam for added personal protection. If finances permit, an alternate choice for the lacrosse goalie is to buy ice hockey goalie pants and do some alterations on them.

> **Note** *When the goalie's legs are together, with these pockets there is less space for the ball to go through.*

C. Shin Guards

Most shin guards come with a flap protection for toes (toenails are always getting hit) and there are hard-toed running shoes for added protection. Foam should be added around the arch of the foot area, tucked in the shin guard, like a tongue on a skate, for additional protection. To help absorb the impact of the ball on the leg, tuck some foam inside the shin guard between the plastic and the cloth.

D. Hockey Knee Pads

Sometimes it is necessary to go down for shots (depending on style), so knee pads for quad and knee protection should be worn at all times.

E. Shoulder Pads

Use ordinary lacrosse player shoulder pads and attach the large kidney pad fibers (from the ordinary player's kidney pads) upside down to the shoulder and bicep area for more protection over the padding. Be sure to strap or tape the fiber to the whole arm to ensure that the equipment will stay in place. It is especially important for younger players to wear this extra fiber protection because a younger goalie will become frightened of the ball if he gets hurt too often. Some goalies like to tie the shoulder pads to the pants to help keep the pants up and the chest protector intact if braces are not desired.

F. Belly Pad and Chest Protector

Try to get a soft, but protective belly pad to aid in absorbing rebounds. The belly pad should be completely flat, not curved; it acts like a wall in providing more area to stop the ball.

Attach the plastic strip (from the ordinary player's kidney pads) on the shoulder part of the chest protector to help absorb shots. A flap of compressed foam could be sewn on the side of the chest protector to protect the kidney area. When getting dressed, some goalies like to tuck the chest protector inside the pants to get rid of the bulkiness, while others like to wear the chest protector outside the pants. Some goalies like to tie the braces together to stop them from sliding down over their shoulders and to help keep their chest protector flat. Most goalies now use a belt-like system to keep their pants up and to keep their chest protector flat to see the ball better when it's around their feet.

Note   *Shoulder pads and chest protector are now one piece.*

G. Elbow Pads

Elbow pads or lacrosse slash guards should be worn to protect the elbows in case of falling.

H. Helmets

Field helmets seem to be the choice of most older goalies. At the younger level, goalie helmets must be approved since it is illegal to wear field helmets. Make sure a throat guard is worn and securely attached at all times, and that the helmet fits snugly and is comfortable.

I. Mouthguard

It is recommended that an internal mouthguard be worn. This is essential for the protection of the teeth.

J. Gloves

Use gloves specially designed for lacrosse goalies by STX for the best protection. For the free hand, because the goalie should use the back part of the hand as a blocker, put some fiber and compressed foam on the inside of the glove to absorb the impact. For the stick hand, put some fiber or foam around the thumb and wrist area.

> **Note** *During practice it is a good idea to wear fibers on the outside and back of both the glove hand and stick hand for additional protection.*

K. Stick

The stick is used for stopping shots as well as passing.

1. Length

A long handle is better for lever action on the pass, but a goalie does not want it too long because the stick then gets caught in the netting of the goal. Find the point on the shaft wherever the stick is balanced. This will help give the goalie an area to grab when passing. If the goalie finds the stick is "head heavy," the stick is too short. The wooden stick gives a goalie a better feel and weight to throw level passes, whereas with the plastic stick he must adjust his release because it has a tendency to produce a higher arc when throwing.

2. Width

a. The Wooden Goalie Stick

> **Note** *The wooden goalie stick is only permitted in the C.L.A. A goalie has the option of using the wooden goalie stick or the plastic kind.*

The saying, "The wider the stick the better," is not always true. A wide wooden stick (15-inch/38-cm inside width) will cover more of the net and thereby help in stopping shots, but it will definitely be a hindrance in passing.

It seems the 15-inch-/38-cm-width goalie stick has become the most common stick on the market today. But for true fast-break goalies, a 13- to 14-inch (33- to 35.5-cm) inside width is best, because they are interested as much in starting the fast-break as they are in stopping the shots, and the smaller and lighter head gives goalies more speed, quickness, and accuracy in their passes.

The youth's wooden goalie stick is a standard 13-inch (33-cm) inside width.

b. The Plastic Goalie Stick

> **Note** *The plastic goalie stick is the only stick permitted in the N.L.L*

The standard plastic goalie stick is approximately 12 inches (30.5 cm) wide, and because it is lighter and smaller, both adults and young goalies use it to improve their passing.

3. Depth

a. The Wooden Goalie Stick

Usually, the depth of the pocket of the wooden stick is about a ball-width below the frame. The trade-off with the shallower pocket is that there is less winding up to throw, resulting in an easier and quicker pass, but more chance of rebounds because of less cushioning of the shot with this type of netting. The trade-off with a two-ball-depth pocket, which is deeper than normal, is that it will help to absorb shots (keeping the ball in the netting and thereby preventing a rebound); however, this deep pocket will present a problem in throwing since a goalie must take a bigger windup to throw the ball, resulting in a slower release and possibly less accuracy.

> **Note** *The goalie wants to form, with the runners, a triangular-shaped pocket in the middle of the netting.*

Approximately two to four shooting strings seem to be normal for goaltenders to help get the proper arc on a pass. Each player will have to experiment to find what is most comfortable for himself.

b. The Plastic Goalie Stick

Goalies have found that with the smaller plastic stick they can get away with making a deeper pocket than the wooden stick pocket without much hindrance in their ball handling.

4. Tape

Tape the shaft of the stick from the throat to 6 inches (15 cm) up the shaft, where the stick is gripped with the stick hand when stopping shots, and from the butt of the stick to about 6 inches (15 cm) down, where the stick is held with the bottom hand when passing. Some goalies even tape the middle of the shaft where they would hold the stick with the top hand for passing.

During the course of the game the wooden or aluminum shaft becomes slippery from the goalie's sweat, resulting in the stick's twisting easily in the hand when passing or stopping shots. The tape helps the goalie grip better and prevents this spinning motion. Change the tape often during the season.

> **Note** *It is important to remember after every game and practice to "air out" the goalie equipment until it is completely dry or it will rot from too much moisture.*

III. "Ready Stance" for a Goaltender

This ready stance is so called because the goalie is balanced and relaxed, yet ready to react quickly. He is in the best stance to move forward, backward, and laterally (side-to-side). Since this stance covers as much of the net as possible, it is important that the goalie stay in this ready stance at all times when the ball is in the Defensive Zone.

*Photo 66:
Ready stance
for a goaltender
(front).*

Photo 67:
Ready stance
for goaltender
(side).

A. Stance *(See Photos 66, 67)*

The goalie takes a crouching position with knees flexed slightly, back straight, shoulders and chest square to the ball, feet shoulder-width apart, keeping the body's weight on the balls of the feet and holding the stick between and in front of the legs, resting his stick hand on his thigh.

B. Glove Hand

There are three styles of holding the glove hand:

1. The goalie can hold the glove hand to the side of the body, cocked, ready to move and turned with the back of the hand facing outwards while keeping the arm flexed with the elbow out to the side to cover more of the net.

2. The goalie can rest the glove hand on the hip area in a position ready to react.

3. The goalie can drop the hand down and let it hang near the thigh in a natural position.

All positions of the glove hand depend on the goalie's style and what feels comfortable to him.

C. Stick Hand

1. Types of Grip

a. A goalie can grab the stick with the thumb on top and along the side of the bent shaft at the throat (the place where the guard meets the handle), making sure the grip is firm.

b. He can wrap his hand around the stick with the thumb on top of and along the straight shaft with the tip of the thumb at the bend.

> **Note** *Some goalies grab the stick with the thumb in the throat, but with this grip there is always a chance of getting the thumb jammed by a shot. As well, with this grip a goalie has a tendency to drop the stick shoulder, depending on his size. It is very important to have both shoulders square to the ballcarrier's stick.*

c. Some goalies wrap the hand around the stick, and wrap the thumb around the shaft rather than along the top of the shaft. With this grip a goalie will not have as firm control over the stick as the other grips, but he will be able to make his stance straighter, and not be bent over.

2. Placement of the Stick Hand

a. Wooden Goalie Stick

The adult wooden goalie stick netting is approximately 24-25 inches (61-63 cm) high. Most goalies can grab the shaft at the throat and have the stick touching the playing surface while maintaining the goalie's stance: knees bent, legs shoulder-width apart, shoulders square over the feet, and stick arm straight or slightly bent. The goalie may have to adapt to keep his stick on the floor by moving his hand up slightly on the shaft, but he may lose some control over his stick with this hand position. Some goalies even move the hand up and down the shaft to maintain the stick on the floor permanently. If the stick is on the floor all the time, a goalie will be stiff and rigid. The stick should be kept on the floor until the shooter takes his shot; then the goalie moves his stick accordingly. *(See the section on "Using the Stick for Stopping Shots" on p. 176)*.

The netting of a child's wooden stick is approximately 20-21 inches (51-53 cm) high from tip to throat and should not present any problem for a youngster gripping the stick at the throat area.

b. Plastic Goalie Stick

The plastic stick's throat is much lower than that of the wooden stick. The plastic goalie stick netting is approximately 18 inches (46 cm) high from tip to throat. If a player grabs the plastic stick at the throat and still keeps the stick on the floor, he will be put off balance by leaning too far forward. To prevent this, players put taped-knobs around the shaft of the stick, about 7-8 inches (18-20 cm) up on the handle from the throat, as a reference point to grab behind or actually grab, to help them keep the stick on the floor and still maintain a good stance. Put the knob at the best spot where it is comfortable and balanced (i.e., in a crouched position which does not require bending over at the waist too much, so that the shoulders are square to the ball and the stick is on the floor).

IV. Goaltending Principles

A goalie has to learn the basic mechanics of goaltending before he can develop his own style. Most goalies learn about goaltending from watching older goaltenders whom they try to imitate, or through trial and error, teaching themselves rather than learning directly from a coach.

Basically, there are two parts to goaltending: the reflexive and the angular.

A. The Reflexive Part of Goaltending

The reflexive part of goaltending relies heavily on the goalie's lateral reactions to get his body — a leg, an arm, or the stick — in front of shots. It also relies on anticipating the shot from years of experience and from knowing the shooter or the situation. *(See section on "Qualities of a Goaltender," p.197.)*

> **Note**   *The goalie practices getting his stomach in front of the ball on every shot as this will help develop the lateral motion that is so important in stopping the ball.*

B. The Angular Part of Goaltending

The angling part of goaltending relies on good body positioning in the crease by stepping out and cutting down most of the net area, leaving the shooter little or nothing to shoot at.

C. Styles of Goaltending

The pure "reflex" goaltender thinks he can react more quickly than the ball, so his basic principle is to set the shooter up by "giving" a part of the net then "taking away" that part of the net as he shoots. He does this by luring the shooter to aim wherever he wants him to shoot by giving him a tempting target (i.e., an open area of net which is usually the short side of the net), then he takes it away by stepping in front of the shot. *(See section on Reflex Goaltender, p. 193.)*

The pure "angle" goaltender does not cheat or guess, but plays the shooter's stick straight on. His positioning is such that the space between the net and both sides of this body is the same. He is so sure of having a good position he rarely moves on a fake because he believes a shooter has to make a great shot to score.

The "standard" goaltender who combines both the reflexive and the angular techniques has to rely on both stepping out, getting good position, and stopping shots with the body or the stick by moving laterally or stepping sideways.

Some goalies may be stronger at playing the reflexive game because of the quick reactions, and some may be stronger at playing the angle game because of their size and ability to take a good position before a shot. But no matter what style a goalie plays, to be good he must be strong in both the reflexive and angular techniques to stop shots. As he becomes more experienced, each goalie will develop his own personal style.

V. The Reflexive Part of Goaltending for Stopping Shots

Goalies try to stop every shot from their ready stance, but they still need the reflexive part of goaltending in stopping shots. From the ready stance, goalies have to react laterally to get something in front of the ball, whether it's their body, the stick, an arm, or a leg. If they start to drop or flop it is because they are out of position, or have made a mistake and have to recover with a spectacular save, or are just tired.

A. Being Out and Set in a "Ready Stance" for Stopping Shots

By being "out and set" (stopped) in a ready stance before the shot occurs, a goalie is ready to move laterally (either way, short side or long side). He must always remember that he cannot rely strictly on angles to stop the ball; no matter how well he plays the angle, there are still many openings. Good players will not aim for the goalie but for these openings, so the goalie still has to rely on his reflexes to stop shots. A major problem for goaltenders is getting caught in transition — they're still moving out when the shot is taken, and are unable to move laterally when moving forward.

B. Using the Stick for Stopping Shots

The stick is the main weapon used to stop long, low shots. Always keep the stick between the legs, in front of the feet, and on the floor, because it spreads out the legs farther, thereby covering more of the net. All shots below the waist on both stick and glove side should be played only with the stick. To cut down on rebounds, the goalie "cushions" the ball by moving his stick backwards as the ball makes contact with the netting. The goalie is more sure of catching the ball with his stick than deflecting it with his glove hand or shin guard.

Usually, low shots are played on the stick side with the stick backed up by that leg (by stepping sideways) and low shots on the off-stick side are played by moving the stick to that side, backed up also by that leg moving sideways. It is important to step sideways as the goalie brings the stick over to block the shot so the leg will act as a brace for the stick and stop it from twisting on the shot. A goalie must maintain a firm grip to have control over his stick, or else the hard shots can turn the stick in his hand and the ball could end up in the net. When the goalie has to make a stick save from a hard low shot without the leg for a backup, he must turn the stick into the direction from which the shot came.

Note   *When using the stick to stop the ball, think of "catching" the ball, to start the fast-break, rather than just stopping the ball. Also, as the low shot comes, the goalie tries to step to the ball as he saves it with his stick, so he is already in the throwing motion to start a fast break.*

C. Using the Upper Body for Stopping Shots

Most saves are made with the upper body. In stopping high-corner shots there are three methods used:

Method #1:
The goalie tries to stop all high shots in the center of the chest, following the principle of keeping as much of the body as possible in front of the ball. However, it is only possible to move the chest one foot (30 cm) in either direction, so shoulders are backups to take away top corner shots until the chest can get over to cover this area. With these high shots on either side of the body, the goalie steps out slightly and steps sideways to get the chest in front of the shot. On the step sideways, his foot will leave the floor with both shin guards facing the shooter. *(See Photos 68, 69.)*

Photos 68, 69:
Using the Upper Body to Stop Shots
Stance and the sideways step against a shooter cross-ing from glove to stick side.

If the shooter moves in tight around the crease, he will generally move in the direction of his stick side. The goalie will maintain his position between the ball and the net. If the goalie ends up moving right over tight to the far goal post, he has to be conscious of the shooter shooting back for the near top corner. In this case, the goalie has to be ready to move back laterally to that particular side to take away the top corner with his upper chest *(see Photos 70, 71, and section on "Positioning for Playing Close-In Shots" on p. 188)*.

Photos 70, 71:
Using the Upper Body to Stop Shots

Stance and sideways step against a shooter crossing from stick to glove side.

High shots that are in the middle of the net are easy to stop with the chest, but "cushion the ball by "giving" or moving back with the chest to cut down on rebounds.

Method #2:

The goalie starts with his shoulder first, then his body. He gets in front of the shot with his chest by stepping over laterally. He keeps his feet on the ground to push off with the stationary foot while stepping sideways with the foot in the direction he wants to go. On the step this leg's shin guard will face the boards. When moving laterally, he stays on his feet.

Method #3:

The goalie takes a stance like a scare-crow, with both elbows out and bent at 90 degrees. He steps sideways in the direction of the shot, but this time he merely stops the shot with the protruding elbow or flicks the arm out straight to block the corner area of the net.

> **Note**   *Beginners have a tendency to turn their body on shots, with the ball hitting their side or their back. Coaches must give them confidence that they can't get hurt through drills and make sure they are well protected.*

D. Using the Upper Body against a Stick-Fake

The goalie facing a stick-fake by a shooter stays square to the shooter's stick relying on his angles (positioning). The key is to have patience and not over-commit. Always let the shooter make the first move; wait out the fake. Many shooters who use fakes find that when a goalie does not commit, but stays square, they will often second-guess themselves and end up either shooting at the goalie or missing the net.

On a fake to the glove side (where the majority of shots will be aimed because it is supposed to be his weakest side), the goalie should not swing his stick up to block a shot. The shot may be a fake, leaving the shooter with the open net on the stick side or low in the feet area. Instead, he should step sideways and up with his body and glove-hand shoulder ready to block the shot while keeping his stick between his legs in the ready stance. If it is a fake, he still has the shoulder on the stick side to come back and make the stop. The goalie should know the types of shooters he is going against so he can anticipate what they like to do. A goalie should be ready for "automatic" moves — if the shooter fakes the goalie up, the goalie should know he is coming down. *(See section on "Positioning for Playing Close-In Shots," p. 188.)*

> **Note**   *Beginning goalies will react to fakes, but good body position will compensate for this overcommitment. Beginners have to fight the tendency to tighten up or blink on a fake. Stay relaxed. Also, be patient by "waiting out" the shooter.*

E. Using the Legs for Stopping Shots

Most often the goalie has his stick between his legs and makes the stick save on low shots. The legs are basically to back up the stick saves, but occasionally he will use a leg as a reflex move to kick a shot away from the net. The one exception occurs when a shot is taken from the side of the net, a goalie can keep one leg tight against the post with both legs close together and the stick at his side.

F. Using the Glove Hand for Stopping Shots

Recall that low shots on the glove side should be played with the stick. It is easier to catch a ball with the stick than to deflect it with the back of the glove. But occasionally the goalie may have to use the glove hand as a blocker for stopping waist-high shots on the glove-hand side of the net.

VI. The Angular Part of Goaltending for Stopping Shots

Definition of "playing angles": The goalie moves out from the net towards the ball to take a position in the crease for the purpose of cutting down on the shooting area of the net, i.e., the shooter has nothing or very little of the net to shoot at, with the result that the ball hits the goalie or forces the shooter to shoot wide. All goalies should remember that forcing a player to shoot wide, or to hit the post, is part of a successful job and is as good as a save.

To explain "playing angles," think of a triangle formed by two imaginary

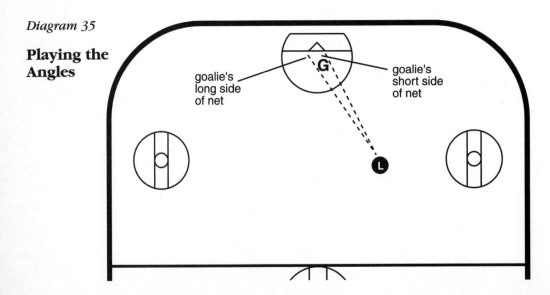

Diagram 35

Playing the Angles

goalie's long side of net

goalie's short side of net

lines from the ball to each goal post. If a goalie plays deep in his net, he will give the shooter more net to shoot at. If the goalie moves out to "challenge the shooter," he will cut down on the amount of net to shoot at. The problem is how to move out *(see section on "Ready Stance for a Goaltender" on p. 171)*, when to move out *(see section on "Being Out and Set" on p. 175)*, and how far to move out *(see this section, Rule #6)*.

REMEMBER: Goaltending is playing angles.

The ideal situation occurs when the ball hits the goalie rather than the goalie having to move to get in front of the shot. So, playing angles is a very important skill in helping to stop the ball. By playing the angles correctly, a goalie can save himself a lot of unnecessary work, but when playing angles a goalie sometimes doesn't take away everything to shoot at, so he must be ready to react and move laterally to protect the rest of the net.

It seems that the most natural shot for shooters is to shoot to their far side (goalie's long side) of the net. It does not matter if it's the goalie's stick side or glove side. If a goalie understands this, in getting his positioning, besides following the principles of "playing angles" he can anticipate this shot more than those aimed for the short side.

Rule #1: *Keep Eyes Centered on the Top-Hand Area*
When the ball is being passed around on the offense, the goalie should keep his eyes on the top-hand area of the players' sticks. He should be focusing on the top-hand wrist, the ball, and the stick, but not on the ballcarrier's body. Some shooters, especially close-in, can get the stick going one way and the ball the other by using their wrists. Some goalies feel it is too difficult to watch just the ball with all this faking, so they watch the top-hand wrist area, and peripherally the ball and the stick's head, to get the overall picture of what the shooter is trying to do. Some goalies get into a bad habit of watching just the shooter's eyes to see if he telegraphs his shot, but good players, knowing this, look one way and shoot the other way.

Rule #2: *Follow the Ball with the Body*
The goalie should not only be following the ball as it moves around with his eyes, but with his body as well, keeping it square to the ballcarrier's stick. So, to keep the proper position, the goalie concentrates on the ballcarrier's stick rather than his body.

Rule #3: *Start All Movement from the Center of the Net*
The goalie should start all movement from a centering position. He does this by standing on the goal line and grabbing both posts with his hands to know where he is and to get his body centered in the net. Some goalies like to grab

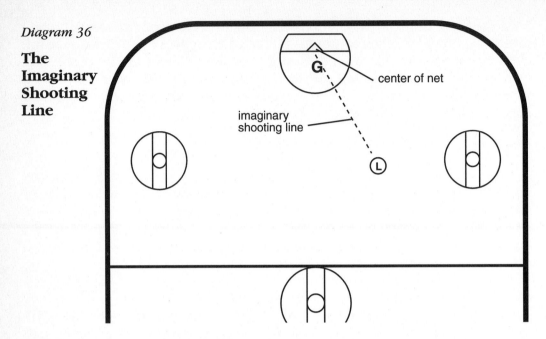

Diagram 36

The Imaginary Shooting Line

center of net

imaginary
shooting line

one post with the free hand and hit the other post with the stick. The idea is that if a goalie knows where he is (centered) before he moves out, he will take a better angle to cut down on the shot.

Rule #4: *Turn the Body on the Goal Line Square to the Stick*

From the center set position on the goal line, the goalie turns to face the direction the ball carrier is coming from. This is called "squaring to the stick." As the ballcarrier crosses the Defensive Zone Line, the goalie turns his body while on the goal line facing the ballcarrier's stick; he then steps out to get his best angle. This procedure keeps the goalie centered in reference to the net as he moves out in the direction of the ballcarrier's stick.

Rule #5: *Move Out on the Imaginary Shooting Line*

The goalie moves out on an imaginary straight line formed with his body, the ball, and the center of the net. By straddling this shooting line he knows there is even space between the net and both sides of this body. He now only has to move one foot either way on a shot. If he moves out off-centered, he will give the shooter too much of the net to shoot at on one particular side (although some goalies do leave one side open to entice the shooter, then by anticipating the shot, take it away).

Rule #6: *Move Out One Step (See Photo 72)*

The goalie centers himself on the goal line, turns his body on the goal line square to the stick, and starts to move out on the Imaginary Shooting Line.

Photo 72:
Ready stance;
one step out.

Now the important question is, "How far should the goalie move out?" A goalie usually takes one step out from the goal line, i.e., "challenging the shooter," to cut down on the amount of net to shoot at, but the distance of stepping out depends on the size of the goalie (adult, one normal step; small adult, a large step; a young goalie, perhaps two steps).

Note   *Because of the larger net used in the N.L.L., a goalie*
has to take an extra half to full step out to cut down
on the amount of net to shoot at.

When the goalie is sure the shot is coming, he can move out another half to one step to take even more net away from the shooter.

Other factors that determine the distance of stepping out include where the ballcarrier is standing, and who is shooting. The goalie takes one step out or comes out as far as he can as long as he can touch the shorter-side post with his glove-hand arm extended, with the end of the shaft of the stick, or with his leg nearest the post extended. Thus he now knows that he is in good position: not too far out, not too deep in his net. All he has to do is take one step back and sideways to get to the far goal post in the event of a diagonal crease pass.

Some goalies move two steps out to get good positioning, but because of variation in size and quickness, goalies will have to do some testing to find out the perfect spot that reduces the shooting area the most. By moving out two steps, a goalie must be aware of recovery back to the far goal post on any cross-floor or diagonal pass. Coming out is important but recovery is just as important. The maximum is two steps. If a goalie takes three steps out, or moves almost to the edge of his crease, the shooter can shoot over a goaltender's shoulder as the shooter's stick is higher than the goalie, or the shooter can cut across in front of the net and shoot around the goalie into the open net. So be careful not to move out too far.

Variation: Another angling method some goalies use is to move out early three steps from the goal line to about the front of the crease as the shooter comes over the Defensive Zone Line. If the offensive player shoots in the area between the two side face-off circles, the goalie is out far enough to cut down the angle and still have time to move on the shot on goal. If the ballcarrier does not shoot and still advances towards the net, the goalie gradually moves backwards one to two steps. If the ballcarrier ends up on the crease, the goalie will have moved back and be stationed about one step out from the goal line and centered in respect to the ballcarrier's stick. The problem with this "coming out and retreating back" method is that the goalie could lose his relationship to the net.

> **Note** *Coaches must encourage young goaltenders to step out and challenge the shooters rather than staying back in their net. Challenging the shooter not only cuts down on the shooting area, but also puts the goalie closer to the ball, which then does not have a chance to build up velocity and hurt him.*

Photo 73:
Ready stance,
two steps out.

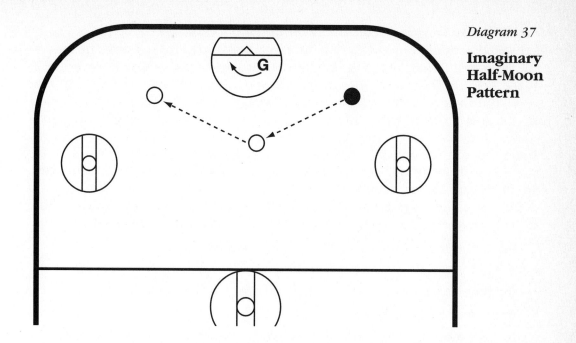

Diagram 37

**Imaginary
Half-Moon
Pattern**

Note   *Young goalies are not as tall as the net and often players score over their shoulders. This is acceptable
because it is better to groom young goalies to play
properly so when they get older they will have good
technique.*

Rule #7: *Trace Out a Half-Moon or Arc Pattern When Moving
Across the Net*

The movement pattern for a goalie in the crease is usually the shape of a half-
moon or arc from post to post. Following this imaginary half-moon or arc pattern gives a goalie a basic position to follow as the ball moves around. As the
ball is moved from one side of the floor to the other, the goalie shuffles in
this half-moon pattern, staying in the ready stance, taking small side steps
with both shin guards facing outwards, keeping his body facing and square
to the ball and keeping his stick along the floor. He takes one step off the
goal post, one side step to the middle of the net, and one side step back to
the other goal post.

A young goalie will take two steps forward off the post, two side steps
(with both shin guards facing outwards) across the top of the half-moon or
arc, and two steps back to the other post (see Diagram 37 above).

Rule #8: *Use Reference Points to Find the Ideal Position*

If a goalie does not know where he is in relationship to his net once he moves out, he is at a disadvantage in knowing what part of the net he is covering. A goalie needs reference points to tell himself if he is in the best spot to cut down the angle and still recover quickly backwards to the net. His best friends are his goal posts. When farther out, he uses the top or "butt end" of his goal stick to find the nearest post to tell himself where he is. A goalie has to know where he is in relationship to the net, especially when he's out from the goal line and in front of the net where he cannot touch the goal posts and does not have time to turn around.

To determine his position, the goaltender can also use the markings on the arena floor as reference points by aligning his body with them, such as:

*   the outer edge of the left and right side face-off circles

*   the left and right side face-off dots

*   the inner edge of the left and right side face-off circles

*   the center face-off circle

It is not a good idea to use the crease as a reference point in getting his proper angle since most times he will be focusing out in front of his net with little time to look down.

Rule #9: *Position of Body in Regards to Specific Positions of Ball*

The references in this section will be for a right-handed goalie (one who holds the stick in his right hand).

Photo 74: Goalie's positioning when the ball is in the corner area.

Most of the game is spent moving forward, backward, and sideways in this half-moon pattern following the ball. Every time the ball moves, the goalie must move to be in the best spot when the ball is shot. It is important that, as he moves, the goalie always stays in his ready stance with his stick on the floor.

1. Position When Ball is in Corner Area of Floor *(See Photo 74)*

The goalie places his outside foot against the nearest goal post with his body and leg hugging tightly to it. His outside arm or stick are on the outside of the post. His inside leg is slightly forward, off the goal line. He stays in the net with his body facing outwards. He should always be checking in front of the net area to see where the opposing players are and what is going on, anticipating what is going to happen, such as a quick pass out and shot.

2. Position When Ball is in Goalie's Right Side Face-Off Area

The goalie steps away from the post at an angle to play the ball honestly — the body stays square to the stick and ball. He first steps out with his inside foot to line up his foot with the stick and ball, then shuffles his outside foot to square up to the shooter. If he can hit the post with the shaft of his stick, with his glove hand, or with his leg nearest the post, this will tell him where he is and that he is in good position when the ball is in the face-off area.

3. Position When Ball is in Front of Net

The goalie is standing one step out from the goal line either by stepping straight out from the center set position or taking one side step from the position when facing the side face-off circle. This is a very difficult position to play because the goalie does not have the goal posts to use as reference points. He should pick other reference points to maintain his floor awareness. He should always know how many steps are needed to get back to his net or to get to the post. If he knows a shooter is winding up for a shot, he should take another step out to challenge the shooter and cut off more of the net.

4. Recovery Move When Ball is Passed Across Floor

Following Rule #2 for playing angles *(p. 181)* — as the ball moves the body moves. The goalie, after taking the one step out from the post, gets in a ready stance to play the ballcarrier *(Photo 75)*. On a quick pass across, he steps back to the far post as a recovery move in case of a quick shot rather than the normal move of stepping sideways around the imaginary half-moon *(Photo 76)*. If there is no quick shot, he steps out again to play the ball square.

5. Positioning for Playing Long-Ball Shooter Cutting Across

Goalies should come one step out from the goal line and stay square to the

Photos 75, 76:
Recovery Move
Play the shooter square, step back to the far post.
(See also Diagram 38, opposite.)

shooter, following him across in front of the net by doing small side steps. Keep the feet shoulder-width apart with the stick between the legs to be in a position to go back the way he came by pushing off with the opposite foot.

6. Positioning for Playing Close-in Shots

a. When shooter is coming across in front of net
The goalie starts on the post and as the shooter comes out from the side of

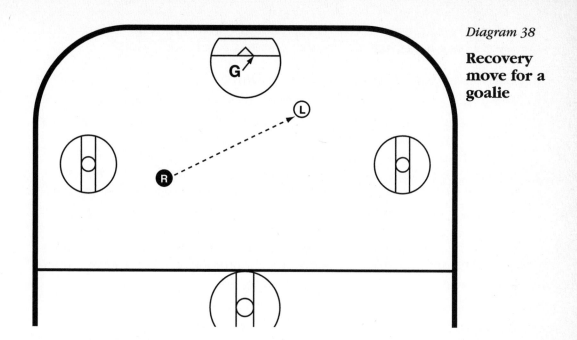

Diagram 38

Recovery move for a goalie

the crease, he follows him across the net. The position is about a half to one full step out from the goal line. If the goalie gets out too far, the shooter can put the ball over his shoulder. He should stay a little closer to the net than when playing the long-ball shooter. Most shooters like to reach around (goalie's long side) or fake to the long side and feed the ball back to where they came from (goalie's short side). A goalie must anticipate these moves. The good angle goalie plays the shooter's stick square and is in his ready stance poised to react accordingly. *(See Photos 68-71.)*

b. When shooter is coming down side of floor
The goalie still follows the principles of coming out, being set, and being ready to move laterally; but as the shooter comes closer to the net, the goalie must shuffle backwards to maintain his proper positioning. If the shooter carriers the ball down the side towards the goal line extended, or if the shooter cuts in towards the net from the side, the goalie might have to attack by stepping into the shot. The key is to step out, not when the shooter is drawing his stick back, but just as he begins bringing his stick forward.

7. Positioning for Playing Long Bounce Shots

The key is to attack the ball by stepping forward and getting out in front of the bounce. First, the goalie must try to catch the ball with the stick before it bounces. If he misses the ball, at the spot it hits the floor or just after it bounces, he puts his body in front of the ball to stop it with either his shin guards or his chest protector. He should not just stab at the ball with the stick, but have a back-up: either the body or the legs together.

8. Positioning for Playing Breakaway Shots

a. The goalie starts from his center set position on the goal line.

b. He waits until the ballcarrier comes into the Defensive Zone, then turns his body on the goal line square to the ball and moves out his one normal step along the Imaginary Shooting Line. The goalie works on the principle of playing the shot as it comes. So, he should be a comfortable distance to play a long shot or to retreat quickly to play a close-in shot.

c. By moving out to eliminate the long shot option, he has forced the close-in shot. When moving backwards as the shooter approaches the net for the close-in shot, it is important to maintain a distance between the goalie and the shooter where the shooter still does not have a good long shot.

d. The goalie is now in his ready stance waiting for

    i) A close-in shot or fake: The goalie should anticipate that as the shooter gets closer to the net, the scoring area is reduced so he might rely more on his fake-shot. Most often the shooter wants to fake first. Just hold ground and let him make the first move. The best move against a fake is not to move. Patience is the key! But remain ready to move backwards and/or sideways when the shot comes.

Photo 77: Goalie's positioning when the ball is behind the net.

ii) A cut across in front of the crease: If the shooter's stick passes the mid-point of the goalie's body, the goalie must be ready to step sideways to the far goal post or be aware of the shooter shooting back to the near side in which case he has to move laterally to that side with his upper chest to take away the shot.

iii) The shooter to run past him straight down the side and try to put the ball in behind him: Just step back sideways to the near goal post.

e. The goalie can try to fake the shooter by "giving and taking away" the shot *(see section on Reflex Goaltender, p. 193).*

9. Positioning When Ball is Behind Net *(See Photo 77)*

The goalie can play this position of the ball in one of two ways:

a. He faces the players out in front and watches for the pass coming out front, periodically turning his head side to side to look over his shoulder for the ballcarrier. He keeps his back to the ballcarrier (his back is tight against the cross bar). He is not concerned with intercepting or deflecting any passes, but with watching the play developing or the ballcarrier coming out from behind the net. Playing the ball behind the net this way, his body is always facing the play in a position ready to make the save.

b. He faces the ballcarrier and hugs the cross bar with his chest, holding his stick up to prevent the ballcarrier from completing the pass in front of the net. Goalies who play this way feel more comfortable watching the passer.

There is no right or wrong way to play the ball when it is behind the net. The goalie just does what is comfortable for him.

10. Positioning During a Face-Off

a. The goalie should stand out of the crease or stand with one foot in and one foot out of the crease.

b. He can hold the stick's head in an "up" position as if catching a ball, or he can hold the stick's head in a "down" position as if scooping up a loose ball.

c. The rule is, "A player cannot pass the ball into his own crease." This is why the goalie must stand outside, or with one foot in the crease and one out (in a position to step out of his crease quickly), in case a teammate gets in trouble and wants to knock or pass the ball back to the goaltender.

d. Another rule is, "A goalie must have at least one foot in the crease for him to draw a loose ball back into his crease." He must be ready to react to a situation where a ball comes loose from the face-off. He can then stretch, trap any loose ball with the stick, and pull it into the crease.

e. The other rule a goalie should be aware of is that if he leaves his crease for a loose ball, he cannot go back into his crease with it and that he is fair game for body contact.

Note *In the N.L.L. a player can pass the ball into the crease while the goalie is in his crease.*

Reminders for Goaltenders

- Keep your eyes on the whole picture — top-hand area, top-hand wrist, ball and stick's head of the ballcarrier.
- Start all movement from the center of the net.
- Turn your body on the goal line square to the ballcarrier's stick.
- Move out on the Imaginary Shooting Line.
- Come out at least one step for good positioning (angle).
- Be stopped and in a Ready Stance before the shot.
- Be ready to step back and/or sideways if necessary.
- Wait out the fake.
- Even with good positioning, be prepared to rely on reflexes if necessary.

VII. Types of Shots and Goalie's Expectations

1. The overhand shot can be the most deceptive because the shooter can shoot straight down at the goalie: releasing the ball early and going for the top corner; releasing the ball late and going for the low corner or a bounce shot; or faking and shooting around the goalie. Most of the time with the overhand shot, the goalie should expect the ball coming high.

2. With the sidearm shot, the goalie should expect the ball to come around him (his long side) as it is difficult for the shooter to pull his shot to the short side. The sidearm shot is usually about waist to top-corner height.

3. With the underhand shot, the goalie should expect a ball low and parallel to the floor, and periodically a rising shot.

4. The goalie should expect the over-the-shoulder shot to occur when he has taken away the long side of the net leaving only the short side. Only a few players can execute this shot accurately, so he should know who they are.

VIII. The Reflex Goaltender

The reflex goalie relies heavily on his quickness and reflexes in stopping shots. This goalie's style is a little different from that of standard goalies so he is discussed here separately.

The reflex goalie likes to set the shooter up by luring him into shooting at a tempting target (an open area of the net), then anticipating that the shooter will aim at the given target, he moves laterally to block the open area and hopefully the shot also. He thinks he can react more quickly than the ball, so he relies heavily on his reflexes to get in front of shots. Because he relies on his quick reactions and anticipation of shots, he does a lot of moving, swinging of arms and stick, flopping, and diving.

So, the reflex goaltender's basic principle is that he likes to "toy" with a shooter.

Playing the Long-Ball Shooter

The reflex goalie's positioning with regard to the long-ball shooter is also different from the standard goalie.

When the ball is in the goalie's right side face-off area, the reflex goalie steps away from the post straight out with his outside foot first, then shuffles his inside foot out. This does not leave him square to the shooter.

He steps straight out to cut off the long side angle on his glove side, thereby leaving a little bit more on the short side (stick side) to shoot at — the principle of giving the short side to shoot at, then taking it away. By stepping straight out rather than coming out at an angle, besides taking away the natural shot for a shooter (the larger opening to the far side of the net), he is also in a better position to take away the quick cross-floor pass and shot or the ever dangerous diagonal cross-floor pass to the crease.

When the ball is in front of the net, the reflex goalie overplays the stick by half a step in front of it to take away the shooter's far side shot and "giving" the long ball shooter the short side. The reflex goalie wants to take away the difficult save to the long side and make the easy save coming back to the short side.

Variation: Some reflex goalies give even more of the far side than the near side to anticipate the shot, but this maneuver could be dangerous since they have to move farther to get in front of the shot.

Playing the Close-in Shooter

A reflex goalie's positioning with regard to the close-in shooter is also different from that of the standard goalie:

a. When playing close-in shots where the shooter is coming across in front of the crease, the reflex goalie wants to take away the shot around him to the long side, by staying about half a step in front of the shooter's stick so the shooter has to come back to the short side, on which the goalie should now anticipate this shot. Basically, the goalie is telling him to shoot at the short side by taking away the long side.

b. When playing the close-in fake shot or playing the breakaway, as already stated, reflex goalies like to "toy" with the shooters by always keeping them guessing what they are going to do. The shooter questions whether the opening is there because the goalie does not know he's left an opening. This gives the reflex goalie an advantage because each time he can play the situation differently: one time he can play the player straight up as a standard goalie; the next time he can play the player on the principle of giving him something to shoot at, then taking it away.

IX. Passing

A fast-break goalie is like a catcher in baseball: defensively, he catches the ball from the pitcher and offensively he must be able to throw the ball quickly and accurately to second base. When a fast-break goalie stops the ball with his stick, he thinks of "catching the ball" rather than just using the stick to stop it. Once he has caught the ball, he is already starting the up motion of the stick to pass. This helps to increase the speed of the the quick outlet pass that is so important on starting a fast break.

The grip for a goalie for passing is similar to the one used by a forward: grasping the stick at mid-shaft and at the end. So, once a fast-break goalie makes a save, he should control the rebound and know exactly what he has to do with the ball. He should look to pass long first, or pass short second to a player around the face-off area.

Note *If he is a ball-control goalie he should look to dump the ball to a teammate in the crease.*

REMEMBER: A goalie has only five seconds in the crease with the ball.

When a fast-break goalie is being pressured while passing, — when an opponent is looking to intercept the pass — the goalie can "pump fake" in one direction and then throw to the opposite direction. This pump fake will "freeze" the opposing player, allowing the goalie time to move sideways and pass unmolested.

Note *It is a good idea for a young goalie to step to the side of the net when throwing a pass, since he might accidentally drop the ball into the net if he stands in front of it.*

X. Loose Balls

When retrieving a loose ball while still in the crease, trap it first, draw it into the crease, scoop it up, then pass it to a teammate. If a goalie has good ball-handling skills and the confidence to leave his crease to obtain a loose ball, his team will have a great advantage as this move of leaving the crease could cause many odd-man situations as he will usually draw a defender and then can "dump off" the ball to a teammate.

XI. Major Goaltending Tips

A. Be Mentally Ready

Anticipate what is going to happen before it happens by "reading and reacting to" the situation, rather than just reacting or guessing. Quickness of mind is an extremely important asset for a goalie.

B. Be Physically Ready

Be in a Ready Stance — knees flexed, body crouched, staying on the balls of the feet, shoulders and chest square to the ball and over the knees, stick between the legs and on the floor — before a shot is taken. When moving, stay in the Ready Stance as much as possible for balance and to move quickly both laterally and forward and backward.

C. Concentrate

Focus on the overall picture, centering on the top-hand area, and peripherally seeing the ball in the stick's head, but not focusing on the ballcarrier's body.

D. Positioning

Know your relationship to the net and to the ball:

1. Center the body in the net, turn the body on the goal line square to the stick, then move out on the Imaginary Shooting Line.

2. Take one step out to "challenge the shooter" and to cut down the area of the net.

3. Keep the stick on the floor even when moving. A shot may bring the stick off the floor.

4. Move the body as the ball moves and keep it square to the ball.

5. Move the body in a half-moon pattern as the ball moves around the floor.

6. Take one step back and sideways to the far post on a quick cross-floor pass (Recovery Move).

E. Playing Low Shots

Catch the low shots with the stick, backed up by a leg.

F. Playing High Shots

Use good lateral movement in an attempt to get the center of the chest in front of high shots, backed up by shoulders and arms.

G. Playing Breakaways

Wait out the fake.

H. Rebounds

Control all rebounds, off the body and off the boards.

I. Passing

Start the fast-break with a quick and accurate outlet pass.

XII. Major Problems in Goaltending

Some of the main problems goalies experience are

- letting his mind wander and losing his concentration on where the ball is and what is happening on the floor;
- not being mentally and physically ready to move laterally to get in front of the shot;
- retreating back into the net too quickly, thereby leaving too much of the net open;
- playing too far out from the net with the result of the shooter cutting

across and shooting around the goalie, shooting over his shoulders, or running straight by him and shooting behind him; and

- losing his floor awareness in regards to the net with the result of leaving too much of one side of the net open.

XIII. Qualities of a Goaltender

A. Physical Qualities

1. Stopping the Ball

Goalies should be good athletes with quick reflexes and good eye-hand coordination. A goaltender cannot be afraid of the ball; this is especially true for beginners.

2. Good Stickhandling Skills

The ability to pass the ball up the floor and the ability to control loose balls and rebounds with his stick are essential. Goalies should be aggressive when going after loose balls around the crease area; when controlling rebounds off their body; when throwing the ball quickly up the floor; when running with the ball up the floor; and when running with the ball up the floor to initiate the fast break.

3. Verbal Communication

The goaltender should tell his teammates where they should play on defense and where the ball is on the floor. He should yell at players for lack of effort; cheer encouragement to players for great efforts and great plays; and keep communication open on the floor between himself and his teammates. All this vocal communication makes the goalie a leader on the team and helps keep him mentally in the game.

B. Mental Qualities

1. Attitude

A goalie has to have a positive attitude, because the way he thinks is the way he plays. he knows that goals will be scored, mistakes will be made, bad calls will be made, and games will be lost, but as long as he does his best nobody can blame him. He must maintain a smile and a sense of humor throughout all adversities.

He must have an attitude of great confidence, bordering on cockiness, in his ability to stop the ball and, especially, in his ability to make the "big save" at crucial times in the game. Making the big save, besides giving his team a lift, maintains the goalie's leadership role.

2. Concentration

In a game, a goalie must focus on the ball and yet be aware of everything going on around him. He has to stay mentally alert every second of the game. He has to tune out all distractions from his mind except what he has to do. He has to focus on the present and not worry about the past (the last goal scored against him) or the future (who will win). When a goalie is "on his game" his thoughts and his actions are one; everything seems to "be in slow motion" where he knows what is going to happen before it happens rather than everything "speeding up," where he reacts or guesses and ends up "fighting the ball."

a. The goaltender can do a play-by-play to help himself stay focused.

b. The goalie can talk to himself: "I will watch the top-hand area and the ball," "I will not over-react to a bad goal or bad call by a referee," "I will challenge all shooters," I love playing against great shooters," "I will take great positioning in the crease," "I will stay mentally alert," "I love pressure and tight situations."

c. He can give verbal instructions to his teammates: "Pressure your man," "Man in front," "Cutter," "Shot."

d. He can break the game into five-minute segments of total concentration.

e. He can count the number of passes by his team in the Offensive Zone.

f. He can follow the rule that when the ball is in the Offensive Zone, this is "the goalie's time": he does things that help him keep loose, such as walking around in his crease, adjusting his equipment, coming out of his net in case any loose balls come back down the floor. But when the ball comes into the Defensive Zone, this is the "coach's time"; the goaltender plays the ballcarrier as if he is going to shoot the ball from anywhere, and follows the ball all the way into the scoring area.

3. Anticipation

Goalies have to learn to read a situation, rather than just react to a situation, and then make a quick decision.

They must understand the whole concept of the game of lacrosse, usually through experience, to help anticipate what could happen. For instance, they must realize that most goals are scored from offensive plays initiated out in front of the net rather than being initiated from behind the net or from the corners. They must realize that there are hardly any deflections or screen shots in lacrosse.

To help anticipate, a goalie must know the opposition beforehand so he knows what to expect. He must know what type of player the ballcarrier is — playmaker or shooter — in order to anticipate what to expect from him.

He can read visual cues from the opponents' actions to help him anticipate. He can watch the ballcarrier's eyes to get an idea if he is going to shoot or pass. If there is eye contact between the ballcarrier and another teammate, the goalie can anticipate a pass-and-cut play. Similarly, by watching the overall picture of the shooter (i.e., top-hand area, the ball and the stick's head), the goalie can anticipate better what is coming: a shot or a fake.

4. Emotional Control

How he reacts when scored upon will determine a goaltender's success or failure. A goalie must realize that he is going to be scored upon and not let that fact throw him off his game or discourage him. He cannot show any negative emotions because this will be taken as a sign of weakness. He must not reveal he is upset by banging his stick on the floor or through a posture of defeat — hanging his head and dropping his shoulders.

A goaltender must keep his cool when the opposition scores on him, whether it was his mistake or not. When a team does score on him, he must analyze what he did wrong, learn from it, forget about it, and then do something to get his mind off what has happened, such as walking away from his crease; never looking at the ball in the net or the opposition; and starting to concentrate on the next face-off. A lacrosse goalie must understand that he can have 15 goals scored upon him, yet his team can still win the game. Not getting upset helps the goaltender stay mentally in the game and ready for anything; it helps him remain confident for the remainder of the game.

To Stop a Shooter, a Goaltender Must

1. Be prepared for his opponent in order to anticipate his moves and out-think him;
2. Concentrate on the top-hand area to anticipate his moves and out-think the shooter; and
3. Execute his goaltending skills to the best of his ability.

XIV. Preparing for a Game

For a goalie to play well he has to have certain good feelings, such as being physically relaxed, yet energized; being mentally calm, yet alert; being confident and optimistic. To get these feelings a goalie must have a physical and psychological pre-game plan. Here are some techniques a goalie can use:

1. Visualization

He can close his eyes and see and feel himself stopping the ball and playing his best game.

2. Self-Talk

Repeating to himself strong, powerful, positive words that stress how he wants to play and what he wants to do: "I love playing goal," "I have fun playing goal," "I love the challenge," "I am the best," "I am ready and prepared," I play relaxed, daring and aggressively," "I love pressure situations." These words will make him feel relaxed, confident, energized, focused and prepared to play.

3. Deep Breathing

Slow and easy breathing.

4. Relaxation Exercises

Tightening and loosening of muscles.

5. Routine

Some goalies like to be busy up to game time; some walk, stretch, listen to music; some find a teammate and stop shots in an adjoining hallway. Others like to isolate themselves in order to visualize their best performance or prepare a list of opposing players so they can anticipate upcoming opposition moves and shots. The important thing is to find the routine that works for you.

XV. Goaltender Drills

The coach should keep the goalie busy and active during the entire practice, but there are two major times in the practice that are strictly for him: stopping shots and passing.

In the shooting drills for goaltenders, the goalie can work on his angles, on his reflexes, on stopping long shots, on stopping close-in shots, and on his weaknesses.

A. Stretching Exercises

Players can get stretching exercises out of books written on exercises. A goalie should make sure he stretches the groin, the hamstring (back of the upper leg), the quadriceps (front of the upper leg) muscles, and the shoulder area.

B. Agility Drills

Agility is the physical ability to move backwards, forwards, and laterally quickly. Again, these drills can be found in most exercise books.
Some suggestions:

1. Any type of skipping, hopping, or jumping can really help to develop agility.
2. Wave drill: The goalie moves in the direction the coach points, forward and backward, side to side, and down and up, while staying in his Ready Stance. Remember: No more than three steps in any direction.
3. Mirror drill: Goalies are in pairs with one goalie imitating the movements of the other goalie.

C. Structured Warm-Up Drills for Practice and Games

Warm-up shooting helps the goaltender to build up his confidence, get him used to being hit, and to work on his angling and reflexes.

1. Progression of Distance: Team starts far out from goalie and gradually works their way in.
2. Progression of hardness of shots: Don't bomb shots at the goaltender at first, as this warm-up is more for the goaltender than the shooter.
3. Players shoot at a variety of corners, practicing their accuracy rather than their scoring ability.

D. Reaction Drills

1. All players with a tennis ball shoot from about 15 feet (5 m) in succession to work on the goalie's reflexes. *(See chapter 8 on shooting.)*
2. Next, have two players shoot two tennis balls at once to help improve the goalie's quickness.
3. Players turn the net around facing the end boards about three feet (1 m) away. The goalie also faces the boards standing exactly in front of the net. His three teammates standing beside and behind the net with three tennis balls. Each in turn bounce a ball off the boards until all the balls are thrown. The goalie reacts to the balls to try to stop the rebounds off the boards from going into the net.

Note *The coach can make up random shooting drills using tennis balls for younger goalies who duck and shrink on shots because they are afraid of the ball. A tennis ball can't hurt them. All they need is a little confidence.*

E. Drills to Teach Angling

1. The coach ties a rope to both goal posts and at the point where the ball would be in the shooter's stick. The two ropes and the goal line from a triangle. To help goalies understand the importance of angling, one goalie starts at the goal line to show how much a shooter can see to shoot at, while another stands where the shooter's stick would be to get the shooting view. The first goalie then moves out, showing the other goal-tender how much of the net he can cut down to shoot at. As he moves out, he practices staying evenly between the two sides of the rope.

REMEMBER: The goalie should not move out too far, as a shot could go over his shoulders very easily.

Variation: The goalie can also show the different positions taken when he centers on the ball versus centering on the shooter's body.

2. The coach can also tape a string in the middle of the net at the goal line and stretch it out to the position of the ball. The string represents the Imaginary Shooting Line. The goalie stands on the goal line centered,

Diagram 39

Finding the ideal spot

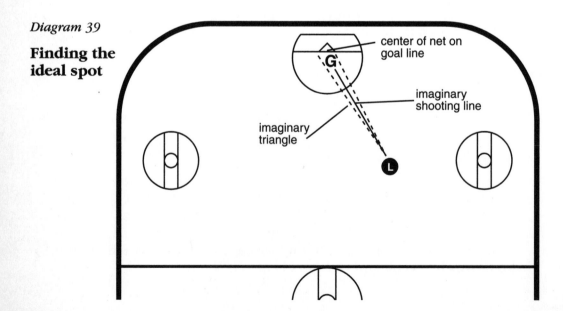

center of net on goal line

imaginary shooting line

imaginary triangle

then moves out on the string representing the Imaginary Shooting Line, staying squared to the ball. The coach gives feedback as he moves in and out.

3. To find the ideal location in the crease for stopping shots, the goalie must

    a. center himself on the goal line;

    b. turn on the goal line square to the ball;

    c. move out one step on the Imaginary Shooting Line.

    Where he stops is his ideal spot for stopping the shot. He can put an "X" on this spot with chalk and take reference points in front of himself.

    Now the goalie stands in his crease in what he believes is his ideal spot and does not move while a player shoots at him. He'll get a sense of his position by the results of the shots — if they go off him or if they go into the net.

4. To help teach angling on the ball, five players each with a ball shoot at the goalie, one at a time, from five different shooting positions. The coach stands behind each shooter to check the goalie's angle. This is a controlled drill.

5. To teach a goalie to move around on the imaginary half-moon line, align five players around the net in good scoring positions. These offensive players pass the ball around slowly and the goalie moves around on his imaginary half-moon line accordingly. The coach checks his position. In the next progression the players pass the ball around, then each takes a shot.

    The goalie, through experience, will get to know his relation to the ball and the net, and his floor awareness in the crease (i.e., his ideal spot).

F. Drills for Stopping Long-Ball Shots

All these drills are the same as the "Shooting Drills" except the purpose is different—they are strictly for the goalie.

    In all these drills the coach will tell the players to take certain types of shots, usually ones that will improve the goalie's weaknesses, or help improve the goalie's stance.

    Types of shots:

-   only long-bounce shots;

-   long shots at the near top corner;

-   long shots at the far top corner;

-   long shots at the near bottom corner;

- long shots at the far bottom corner;
- shooting at any opening;
- shooting at goalie's chest;
- shooting at goalie's stick side;
- shooting at goalie's glove side;
- shooting at goalie's shin guards.

Note   *These drills will also improve the players' shooting accuracy. They can be run either in a controlled manner where the shooters are spaced out to give the goalie time to get set between shots so he can work on his technique, or at a high speed where the shooters fire continuously one after another so the goalie does not have time to get set and thereby works on his quickness and reflexes.*

1. Individual Shooting Drill

Individual shooter shoots from the crease area, the corner area, or from the middle of the floor. He shoots repeatedly at a specific spot indicated by the coach. The passer has a bucket of balls from which he feeds the shooter.

2. Breakaway Long Shot Drill

Players line up at the center face-off circle and run in on the goalie. The goalie can make the drill more difficult on himself by not using his stick.

3. Single Line Drill

Players cut down the side or cut across the top. The goaltender works on his angling and positioning.

4. Semi-Circle Long-Shot Drill

Each player with a ball will line up around the Imaginary Semi-Circle Line. A goalie can work on his angling by staying on his imaginary half-moon, by having the players shoot slowly and continuously; or on his reflexes, by having the players shoot rapidly and continuously; by alternating from side to side of the semi-circle, or by shooting out of sequence (i.e., the players are given a number), then mixed up. When the coach calls out a number, that particular player shoots.

5. Two-Line No-Pass Cornerman Shooting Drill

Players shoot around a pylon in the middle of the floor. Players can alternate sides so the goalie can work on his reflexes, or all the players on one side can shoot so the goalie can work on his angling. Again, the goalie should practice stopping shots with or without his stick. *(See chapter 9, Shooting.)*

6. Merry-Go-Round Drill

A goalie can work on his reflexes by having the drill run quickly, or he can work on his angling by running the drill slowly. *(See chapter 9, Shooting.)*

G. Drills for Stopping Close-In Shots

Same as the above drills. Types of shots:

- Shooting close-in shots with no fake to the far side.
- Shooting close-in shots with no fake to the near side.
- Shooting close-in shots with one fake to the near side, then shooting to the far side.
- Shooting close-in shots with one fake to the far side, then shooting to the near side.

1. Breakaway Close-In Shot Drill

(See chapter 9, Shooting.)

2. Two-Line No-Pass Creaseman Shooting Drill

Pylon is placed in front of the net and beside the crease. Players' options: shoot before the pylon; shoot after the pylon. Alternate left side, right side, or run all the rights then all the lefts. *(See chapter 9, Shooting.)*

3. Diagonal Shooting Drill

The goaltender works on stepping, from a position on the shooter in the cornerman's area, to the far goal post to stop the shot from the opposite creaseman who receives a diagonal-crease pass from the shooter.

H. Lateral Motion Drill

Players shoot from both cornermen's positions, who aim for the far top corner. The goalie without his stick must move laterally to stop the shot with his body or upper shoulder and arm.

I. Initiating the Fast Break

Players are in two lines near the end boards on their proper side of the floor. A player from one line rolls the ball to the goalie who practices picking it up and throwing it to the same player who has run to his side face-off circle.

Afterword

I HOPE my suggestions and tips for playing the sport of lacrosse are helpful to players, coaches, fans and parents; and that by using them you will come to enjoy the competition and have as great a love of the game as I have.

As a teacher and coach I always encourage feedback. Should you have ideas or suggestions regarding this book, please contact me in writing care of

Warwick Publishing
162 John Street,
Toronto, Ontario, Canada, M5V 2E5
FAX: (416) 596-1520
E-mail: mbrooke@warwickgp.com

Resources

There aren't many books about lacrosse, especially box lacrosse, which is one of the reasons I wrote this one. I've also written a second book, *Lacrosse Team Strategies* (ISBN 1-895629-55-1), which builds on the skills described here. If you can't find it at the bookstore, they should be able to order it for you.

There are many lacrosse sites on the Internet. Many focus on field lacrosse but also have useful information for all kinds of lacrosse players. Here are but a few:

www.e-lacrosse.com *An online lacrosse magazine*
http://lacrosse.miningco.com *A lacrosse information page*
www.lacrosse.org *site for US Lacrosse*
www.laxtreme.com *News about pro lacrosse*
www.englishlacrosse.co.uk *Site of the English Lacrosse Association*
http://alc.lax.org.au/ *Australian Lacrosse Council site*

Organizations

National Lacrosse League (NLL)
237 Main St., Suite 1500
Buffalo NY 14203
Tel: (716)855-1NLL/FAX: (716)852-4155
Web: www.be-lax.com

Canadian Lacrosse Association (CLA)
2460 Lancaster Rd., Suite 200
Ottawa ON K1B 4S5
Tel: (613)260-2028/FAX: (613)260-2029
E-mail: info@lacrosse.ca/Web: www.lacrosse.ca

Acknowledgements

Whenwriting this book I approached 18 of the best lacrosse players in Canada to get their feedback on the skills of the game of lacrosse. With their input they added those extra-special ingredients that will help make players, coaches, and parents understand the execution of these skills.

I would like to acknowledge the following people for their time, energy, and contribution to this book:

Passing and Catching: Terry Lloyd, Jim Wasson, Gaylord Powless, Ed Derks, Ron MacNeil.

Long Ball Shooting: John Fusco, Larry Lloyd, Jim Meredith (Assistant Coach, Buffalo Bandits), Derek Keenan, Kevin Alexander.

Close-In Shooting: Special thanks to Terry Lloyd, Peter Parke, Ed Derks.

Individual Offense: Terry Lloyd, Jim Wasson, Ed Derks, John Fusco, Gaylord Powless.

Face-offs: Gordon Purdie (New York Saints), Jim Wasson, Gaylord Powless, Elmer Tran, Derek Keenan (Assistant Coach, Toronto Rock), Kevin Alexander. Special thanks to John Fusco for the basis of this chapter, and referee Bill Fox of the O.L.A. and N.L.L.

Goaltending: Bob Watson (Toronto Rock), Gee Nash (New York Saints) Shawn Quinlan, Merv Marshall, Ken Passfield, Ted Sawicki (coach of the Buffalo Bandits), Doug Favell, Bucky Crouch. Special thanks to Barry Maruk on Reflex Goaltending, and to Wayne Colley on Angle Goaltending and the extra time he spent on helping refine this chapter.

In addition, the contributions of the following individuals were essential: W.T. Westhead for editing the first draft; Mike Keenan for his beautiful introduction; Chief Irving Powless, whose terrific foreword adds a sense of history to the book; Joe Nieuwendyk for reading and endorsing the book; Dieter Hessel for the great instructional photographs and Christine Nastasi for her action shot from the M.I.L.L.; George and Rainier for the use of their facilities at Soccer City in Whitby, Ontario; Derek Keenan, John Fusco, and Wayne Colley for posing for the photographs—three great players who are a credit to the game.

Thanks also to my publisher, Nick Pitt, for believing in the book and being so encouraging and easy to work with. I'm grateful to you all.